The Society For The Destitute Presents
Titus Bouffonius

# The Society For The Destitute Presents Titus Bouffonius

Very loosely based on
William Shakespeare's *Titus Andronicus*

Colleen Murphy

*The Society For The Destitute Presents Titus Bouffonius*
first published 2021 by Scirocco Drama
An imprint of J. Gordon Shillingford Publishing Inc.


Scirocco Drama Editor: Glenda MacFarlane
Cover design by Doowah Design
Cover photo: Peter Anderson as Titus B. – photography by Tim Matheson
Author photo by Heidi Hamilton
Production photos by Tim Matheson

Printed and bound in Canada on 100% post-consumer recycled paper.
We acknowledge the financial support of the Manitoba Arts Council and The Canada Council for the Arts for our publishing program.



Production inquiries to:
Michael Petrasek, Kensington Literary Representation
34 St. Andrew Street, Toronto, ON M5T 1K6
kensingtonlit@rogers.com 416-848-9648

*Library and Archives Canada Cataloguing in Publication*

Title: The Society For The Destitute Presents Titus Bouffonius / Colleen Murphy.
Other titles: Titus Bouffonius
Names: Murphy, Colleen - author.
| Based on (work): Shakespeare, William, 1564-1616. Titus Andronicus.
Description: A play.
Identifiers: Canadiana 20210138521 | ISBN 9781927922774 (softcover)
Classification: LCC PS8576.U615 S63 2021 | DDC C812/.54—dc23

J. Gordon Shillingford Publishing
P.O. Box 86, RPO Corydon Avenue, Winnipeg, MB Canada R3M 3S3

*This play is dedicated to*
*Michael Kennard*
*and*
*The Art of Bouffon*

"*The Society For The Destitute Presents Titus Bouffonius* is deranged, darkly funny, and perverse, but its subversiveness also serves a purpose, and it makes for an unforgettable experience."

— Andrea Warner, *The Georgia Straight*

"*The Society For The Destitute Presents Titus Bouffonius* is strikingly original and delivered with enough verve and 'you-can't-do-that-on-stage' style to take your breath away — while leaving you with lots to talk about after the show."

—- Colin MacLean, *GigCity*, Edmonton

"*The Society For The Destitute Presents Titus Bouffonius* encourages us to get comfortable with discomfort, to revel in the outrageous and to trade our tears for laughter."

— Lauren Donnelly, *Vancouver Weekly*

"There are comedies that are black; there are comedies that are very black. And then there's *The Society For The Destitute Presents Titus Bouffonius*: it's riotously black. All good unwholesome fun."

— Liz Nicholls, www.12thNight.ca

"I can't remember the last time I saw a show that got me so excited I thought I might lose my marbles."

— Colin Thomas, colinthomas.ca

"If you need a really good laugh and you're okay with dark, grisly, bloody, grotesque, rude and crude — all wrapped up in the French clowning style called bouffon — you will love *Titus Bouffonius* as much as I did."

— Jo Ledingham

"This show is smart. The heady mix of bouffon revelry and Shakespearean trauma is fuel for an edgy comedy, and playwright Colleen Murphy has dug deep into both worlds to concoct an experiential feast."

— Chelsey Stuyt, *Vancouver Presents*

"*The Society For The Destitute Presents Titus Bouffonius* at first presents itself as a chaotic project by confused misfits, but in reality it is an intelligent (if not eloquent) commentary on the Shakespearean classic and the complexities of the world which we navigate."

— Ljudmila Petrovic, *SAD MAG*

"*The Society For The Destitute Presents Titus Bouffonius* might give you a lot to talk about the next day…we were all pretty much speechless."

— Tiva Quinn

"The show contains both clowns and Shakespeare...and tampons. Happily, it's all gloriously mashed together in an uproarious send-up of struggling theatre groups and demanding audiences and various taboos, including society's fascination with violence, penned by one of Canada's most celebrated playwrights."

—Liane Faulder, *Edmonton Journal*

# Colleen Murphy

Colleen is a playwright, filmmaker and librettist, born in 1954 in Rouyn-Noranda, Quebec, and raised in Northern Ontario.

Her play *Pig Girl* won the 2016 Governor General's Literary Award for Drama as well as the 2014 Carol Bolt Award. *The December Man / L'homme de décembre won* the 2007 Governor General's Literary Award for Drama, the CAA/Carol Bolt Award and the Enbridge Playwrights Award. Other plays include *The Breathing Hole* (shortlisted for the Susan Blackburn Prize, U.S., and the Carol Bolt Award), *I Hope My Heart Burns First* (formerly *Bright Burning), Armstrong's War, The Goodnight Bird, Beating Heart Cadaver* (shortlisted for the 1999 Governor General's Literary Award for Drama), *The Piper* and *Down in Adoration Falling*. Libretti include *Oksana G.* (c. Aaron Gervais) for Tapestry Opera (nominated for seven Dora Mavor Moore Awards), *Bring Me the Head of the President* and *My Mouth on Your Heart* (c. August Murphy-King) for Tapestry and Toy Piano Composers and Bicycle Opera, respectively. Colleen twice won prizes in the CBC Literary Competition. She is also an award-winning filmmaker and her distinct films have played in festivals around the world.

Colleen has been Writer-in-Residence at four theatres and six Canadian universities and Canadian Playwright-in-Residence at Finborough Theatre in London, UK.

# Acknowledgements

In 2015 the wonderful Stephen Drover, who was Artistic Director of Rumble Theatre in Vancouver at the time, commissioned me to write an adaptation of Shakespeare's *Titus Andronicus*. I thought, "Yeah blood & guts, that's right up my driveway — easy as pie," but I struggled mightily to find the form.

The carnage of the 20th century propelled Shakespeare's revenge play to a greater level of popularity and perhaps a greater level of meaning but, when I read the play again, I had trouble connecting with the notions of honour and revenge that justified the violence. What makes people so angry that they kill children and kill even their own children? What is behind such rage? Hurt probably, and grief. Ask a soldier whose best friend was shot to pieces right in front of them. Ask a parent whose child has been murdered what they do with their grief and rage. Turn anger in on oneself and it's depression; turn it out, it's aggression. Psychology is one aspect, but religion and honour are others. Humans sacrifice people and animals to appease their gods, or purify their community, or return order and familial honour; however, religious and cultural beliefs do not let humans off the hook — killing is killing is killing. My heart broke for all the dead children.

During the time I was adapting the play I was Lee Playwright-in-Residence at the University of Alberta, working in the same department as Associate Professor Michael Kennard, a.k.a. Mump from the incredible horror clown duo Mump & Smoot. I was inspired by the rigour and the fearlessness he used in his seriously hilarious student presentations, and I realized that the form of bouffon would help me smash apart a play about power and empire and give it over to five powerless, dispossessed characters to perform. I asked Michael to help me and I owe the manifestation of this work to him — to his heart and to his expertise. Stephen was incredibly supportive, too, flying to Edmonton to work with Michael and me. Together the three of us discovered how to incorporate the form and work the violence. Violence offers a kind of terrifying thrill to most people, but I wasn't interested in reproducing gory, blood-spurting naturalism in the hopes that an audience member might faint, which is often how a successful production of *Titus Andronicus* is measured. Pretend blood is boring and unconvincing on stage. Ketchup is way more fun!

I owe the creation of this play to these mighty artists: Stephen Drover, Michael Kennard, Sarah Afful, Peter Anderson, Craig Erickson, Pippa Mackie, Naomi Wright, assistant director Kim Senklip Harvey, composer Mishelle Cuttler, and the creative team at Rumble Theatre in Vancouver. Thank you, Sarah, for urging me to confront, head-on, the racism in Shakespeare's text. Thank you times a thousand to Bradley Moss, Artistic Director of Theatre Network in Edmonton, and his artistic team who, in their production, opened up the play to include wild improvisation. Thank you to Helen Belay, Robert Benz, Hunter Cardinal, Bobbi Goddard and Marguerite Lawler for their courage in "going where the fear is." I also want to acknowledge the specific and deeply felt rewriting work that Helen Belay and Hunter Cardinal layered into the "Kill the Nurse" section. Using their own performances and lived experience as reference, they beautifully refocused and strengthened the text and subtext for Fink, his performance of the Nurse, and for Boots. Thank you, Scott and Darrin — I love you guys, and thanks, Tessa.

In the cack-up of the 21st century, bouffon is a perfect form for adapting *Titus Andronicus* because it brings urgency to a bunch of poverty-stricken clowns from the gutters who are acting out their grief and rage and mocking everyone else at same time.

William Blake said that "excessive sorrow laughs." Excessive sorrow also stings.

Colleen Murphy
Playwright-at-Large

# Greetings from the Swamp

The bouffon style was first created by Philippe Gaulier and Jacques Lecoq in Paris in the 1960s. It was designed to help students be more comfortable performing in the grotesque and parody styles (called Point of Attack). Gaulier said, *"Bouffon are the hunchbacks, the lepers, the syphilitics, everyone that society has rejected. But they come to tell us — God's beautiful children — that all aspects of humanity belong to everyone. In the grotesqueness of the bouffon is a truth about Humanity."* The style was created based on the medieval Feast of Fools / Feast of Asses celebrations. On that day the people who lived in swamps and gutters would be invited to come into town to perform for the people in power. The hope of these rejects was to make powerful people laugh at what they had performed, then go home and kill themselves after realizing that they — the people in power — were the cause of all society's ills. The performance was a form of protest.

In the physical comedy world bouffon are known as the children of the devil and clowns are known as the children of God. In the bouffon performance style, charm, intelligence, and parody are used to bring the audience into their world. There is also direct audience interaction that can lead to numerous moments of improvisation; it can be both arresting and soothing at the same time. You never know when one of the bouffon will stop the show and give you a compliment that will leave you reeling in guilt for your contribution to the current condition of humanity.

I first met Colleen in 2014 when she came to the University of Alberta's Drama Department as its new Playwright-in-Residence. Colleen and I had crossed paths indirectly many times in the years before without really knowing or meeting each other. I had read or seen many of her plays, *Beating Cadaver Heart, The Piper, The December Man, Armstrong's War, The Breathing Hole,* all brilliant in their own way. For many years, Colleen and her late husband, filmmaker Allan King, would sneak their young son August into the theatre to see the macabre world of Mump and Smoot. Mump and Smoot had also begun working on a documentary project with Allan just before he died. After many hallway and office chats, it didn't take long for Colleen and me to realize that we both had a penchant for the dark side of things and that in the end...we all die.

About one year into her residency, Colleen mentioned she had been commissioned by Stephen Drover at Rumble Theatre to do an adaptation of *Titus Andronicus* and was wondering what I thought of doing it in the bouffon style. She had seen a few of my physical comedy classes at the university and had become inspired by the bouffon style. I immediately said it was an exciting and risky idea. Over the next two years Colleen, Stephen and I did three different workshops to explore how the style and script worked together. It took some exploring and tweaking until we all felt it was ready to go to full production. We were all scared shitless and wondered what we had gotten ourselves into. Will it work? Will audiences like it? Will we be run out of town on a razor blade?

I have to say we really were scared shitless about what audiences would think. This to me is truly what theatre is about: risk taking. It's about going where the fear is and saying something that you truly believe in. It is especially true in regards to using bouffon as its style. There isn't a lot of bouffon done these days and it can be quite offensive to some. To be quite honest, it takes an incredible amount of skill to pull off as a performer.

Colleen Murphy's delightfully twisted new play *The Society For The Destitute Presents Titus Bouffonius* is about a clump of poverty-stricken people that come together to put on their favourite plays. This time their production is an adaption of Shakespeare's *Titus Andronicus.* The plays they pick become vehicles for what they want to say about humanity, for what they want to protest and, finally, for what all of us involved in production want to express. One of the things I love about Colleen's work is her fearlessness and her ability to take dangerous topics and find a way to make them accessible to audiences and performers.

Needless to say, something worked. The first production, directed by Stephen, was nominated for nine of Vancouver's Jessie Richardson Awards, winning six, including Best Production. Bradley Moss directed the second production of the play at Theatre Network in Edmonton. It garnered nine Elizabeth Sterling Award nominations and won three, including Best Production. Colleen and I would both agree that credit be given to all the risk-taking and fearlessness of both casts, crews and our directors.

I love bouffon because it adds a bit of an edge to everything. It puts the audience on the edge of its seats and makes them really look at what they are doing in their beautiful lives. It is a great reflection on the current state of humanity. I also love bouffon because it has had a huge impact on my work with Mump and Smoot. John Turner (Smoot), Karen Hines (Director), and I all studied bouffon with Gaulier in the 1990s. It helped give us the edge we were looking for in the Mump and Smoot characters and in Karen's neo-bouffon character, Pochsy. It also gave us some wonderful performing and teaching techniques. All the research John, Karen and I did together over the past thirty-five years undoubtedly gave me the opportunity and the knowledge to coach *The Society For The Destitute Presents Titus Bouffonius*. I was fortunate enough to be the bouffon / clown coach on the first two productions (Rumble Theatre and Theatre Network) and I can truly say they were both highlights in my professional career. It is a play that is needed now, a play that makes us cringe, laugh, cry, and reflects back to us who we have become as a society.

I love this powerful play and love watching audiences react to it. I love bouffon because it is a protest on so many levels.

I truly hope you are moved, offended and provoked to make a stand on something you believe in. This world needs that, it needs this play, it needs the bouffon work and it needs Colleen's voice. I thank Colleen for this wonderful opportunity and all she has shared and now, "There will be Pie!"

Michael Kennard
Associate Professor, University of Alberta
Co-Artistic Director, Mump and Smoot

## Production History

*The Society For The Destitute Presents Titus Bouffonius* was commissioned by Stephen Drover, Artistic Director of Rumble Theatre in Vancouver. The play had its world premiere on 24 November 2017 at the Cultch, directed by Stephen Drover. Michael Kennard worked with the actors on the art of bouffon and contributed greatly to the play and to the production. The sets and costumes were designed by Drew Facey, with lighting designed by Sophie Tang and original music composed by Mishelle Cuttler.

BOOTS plays Aaron ................................Sarah Afful

SPARK plays Tamora ...............................Naomi Wright

SOB plays Titus .......................................Peter Anderson

LEAP plays Lavinia ................................Pippi Mackie

FINK plays Saturninus & Bassianus ....Craig Erickson

2018 — Winner of 6 Jessie Richardson Awards including Outstanding Production

The play was subsequently produced in January 2020 by Theatre Network in Edmonton, and directed by the theatre's Artistic Director, Bradley Moss. Michael Kennard worked with the actors on the art of bouffon and contributed greatly to production. Set and costumes designed by Tessa Stamp and lighting designed by Scott Peters. Music and sound design by Darrin Hagen.

BOOTS plays Aaron ................................Helen Belay

SPARK plays Tamora ...............................Bobbi Goddard

SOB plays Titus .......................................Robert Benz

LEAP plays Lavinia ....................................Marguerite Lawler

FINK plays Saturninus & Bassianus ....Hunter Cardinal

2020 — Winner of 3 Elizabeth Sterling Awards including Outstanding Production

Revenge is the sugar in my blood, the acid in my dirty shame: (left) SPARK (Naomi Wright), SOB (Peter Anderson), BOOTS (Sarah Afful) are singing. Photographer Tim Matheson for Rumble Theatre.

Ye white-limbed walls, ye fucking white people, coal black is better than another hue: BOOTS (Helen Belay) chides a Nurse. Photographer Ian Jackson/Epic Photography for Theatre Network.

Master of my life — calm the fuck down: SPARK (Naomi Wright), FINK (Craig Erickson). Photographer Tim Matheson for Rumble Theatre.

O gods we kneel on broken knees: (top left) FINK (Hunter Cardinal), SOB (Robert Benz), (foreground left) LEAP (Marguerite Lawler), BOOTS (Helen Belay), SPARK (Bobbi Goddard) are singing. Photographer Ian Jackson / Epic Photography for Theatre Network.

Call 911— the fuckers cut out my tongue: LEAP (Pippa Mackie) begs audience members for help. Photographer Tim Matheson for Rumble Theatre.

An eye for an eye and there will be pie: (left) BOOTS (Helen Belay), (lying on the table) LEAP (Marguerite Lawler), (foreground) SOB (Robert Benz), (right, on table) FINK (Hunter Cardinal) enjoy a last supper together. Photographer Ian Jackson/Epic Photography for Theatre Network.

# Characters
(in alphabetical order)

BOOTS
A black female, plays Aaron

LEAP
A female, plays Lavinia

FINK
A male, plays Saturninus & Bassianus

SOB
A male, plays Titus

SPARK
A female, plays Tamora

## Time

Today

## Setting

A shabby stage or a playing area of sorts

## Props

Lots of plastic baby dolls to play the children, et al.

Hammer, nails, and a board for the crucifixion

Six red plastic bottles for squirting ketchup

Lots of ketchup (Blood)

Plastic knives and forks (Weapons)

Paper crowns from Burger King (Crowns)

Life-size plastic skeleton from a dollar store (Revenge)

Cheap plastic daffodils

Small bag of loonies (Coins)

A real pie

# Production Notes

Please hire diverse artists for the cast and crew and feel free to customize the text to reflect the specific locale of the production. For example, early on the character Sob mentions, *"We found this old set at the Playhouse and strung up lights and now the big day is here."* Sob is referring to Vancouver Playhouse that closed years ago...so things like this are easily adaptable.

Have fun and, as Michael Kennard says, *"go with the fear..."*

All futurity seems teeming with endless destruction
never to be repelled; desperate remorse swallows
the present in a quenchless rage.

— *William Blake*

*SOB, LEAP, SPARK, FINK and BOOTS enter as a gang, huddled together, smiling but nervous. SOB and SPARK clutch their "doll" children. SOB steps forward.*

SOB: The Arts Educational Outreach for People with Green Noses who write with their Left Hand, People with Boils on their Cheeks, People with Pink Ears and No Feet, People who self-identify as Pineapples and People who live in Poverty gave some of us — the Residents of The Society For The Destitute — a five-hundred-dollar grant to put on a play. Thank you.

BOOTS: Thank you.

SPARK: Thank you.

FINK: Thank you, taxpayers. I love you. I love you most dearly.

SOB: Some of the more artistically inclined residents met in the community lounge every second Wednesday to read plays by William Shakespeare. It was fun.

BOOTS: It was fun.

SPARK: It was fun.

LEAP: It was fun.

FINK: It wasn't.

SOB: We read lots of plays.

LEAP: *Romeo and Juliet.*

BOOTS: *Macbeth.*

FINK: *Titus Andronicus* had the most murders.

SPARK: Thank you, taxpayers.

BOOTS: *(As Macbeth, with a brogue.)* Tomorrow and tomorrow and tomorrow creeps in this petty pace from day to day to the last sylla—sorry.

SOB: Boots.

BOOTS: Sorry.

SOB: We found this old set at the Playhouse and strung up lights and now the big day is here. We only get one day to do our play, only one — and this means so much to us. Before we begin the play — trigger warning — this is for our more traumatized patrons — be warned that our performance may contain a few moments of interpretive dance. Now the players are going to introduce themselves.

BOOTS: My name's Boots. I'm a recovering alcoholic. I like to read books and take long walks on the beach. I wanted to be Macbeth in *Macbeth* but in this play I'm Aaron, who is also the secret lover of Tamora, and I'm one of the Narrators.

SPARK: Hi, I'm Spark. I play Tamora, Queen of the Goths. I guess I'm a recovering mother eh 'coz I'm trying to recover my two kids from fuckin' Children's Aid. The Aid's got 'em imprisoned somewhere in the back of a restaurant. I play a Narrator and Tamora, Queen of the Goths.

SOB: Fink.

*Silence as FINK slowly and grimly makes his way towards an audience member.*

SOB: Fink! Introduce yourself.

FINK: Mostly I watch people play video games like Manhunt, Kill the Rich, Super Columbine. I'm kind of a recovering kid because my mother left when I was five so I'm trying to recover her. She's got short hair and tattoos on her neck. I play two parts — Saturninus, who's the oldest son of the late Emperor of Rome, and Bassianus, who is Saturninus' younger brother. Two parts. And sometimes I play a Narrator.

LEAP: I'm Leap — Lisa Elizabeth Amanda Peters — Leap for short. I'm going to be a veterinarian someday. I like to sing and dance and suck cock when I need money because I'm saving up to buy a rescue dog, hopefully a German Shepherd or a Dalmatian, and I play Lavinia and a Narrator, too.

SOB: And last but not least, me — Sob. I love watching old movies with Laurence Olivier, Alec Guinness and Dirk Bogarde — men with chests. I enjoy the occasional glass of wine and have been out of prison now for four years, seven months, nineteen days and three hours. I shall be playing the part of Titus and sometimes a Narrator. We chose this play because it's about grief, vengeance and the relish of murdering children — your own and other people's.

BOOTS: Thank you, taxpayers.

SPARK: *(As Tamora, holding up her dolls.)* These are my sons Donny, Kevin and Albert.

SOB: *(As Titus, holding up his dolls.)* These are my sons Mikey, Leroy and Todd. Ladies and Gentlemen, we are proud—

LEAP: I'm Lavinia.

SOB: Yeah, sorry — my dear daughter Lavinia. Hello Lavinia.

LEAP: Hi, Daddy.

BOOTS: I want to be Macbeth.

SOB: Next time.

LEAP: Most of these dolls are mine.

SOB: Esteemed Guests — we are proud to present our adaptation of *The Lamentable Tragedy of Titus Andronicus* by William Shakespeare. We call our adaptation *Titus Bouffonius*.

*Music.*

SOB: It's (today's date). The Emperor of Rome has died. Titus, the General of the Roman Army, who won a ten-year war against the Goths — bad and hairy people — returns to Rome with the body of his son and also with a prisoner, Tamora, Queen of the Goths. Let's see what happens.

*LEAP steps forward.*

LEAP: *(As Narrator.)* Two households both alike in dignity in fair Verona where we—

SOB: Wrong play.

BOOTS: Wrong.

FINK: Fucking idiot.

SPARK: Wrong.

*Music stops.*

LEAP: Sorry. *(As Narrator.)* Rome. The Capital of the Roman Empire.

*Music starts.*

LEAP: *(As Narrator.)* The Tomb of the Bouffonii. Lights come up on Titus holding his dead son. His prisoners — Tamora, her three sons, and Aaron— are all in chains.

BOOTS: I'm Aaron and I'm in fucking chains.

SOB: *(As Titus, à la Olivier.)* Hail, Rome, victorious in thy mourning weeds! Lo, as the bark, that hath discharged her fraught, returns with precious lading to the bay from whence at first she weighed her anchorage, cometh Bouffonius, bound with laurel boughs to re-salute his country with his tears. Romans, of my twenty-five valiant sons, twenty were slain in war, one is newly dead, now only four remain — no, sorry — now only three remain. Behold my dead son…be so kind and hold his poor shimmering remains whilst I mourn.

*SOB goes into the audience and gives the doll — a Kleenex over its little face — to an audience member to hold, then he breaks down and weeps inconsolably.*

LEAP: *(As Narrator.)* The tomb is opened.

SOB: Not yet.

LEAP: Not yet. Sorry. *(As Narrator.)* Not yet.

SOB: *(As Titus.)* This son I bring unto his latest home, for burial amongst his ancestors — but first, give me the proudest prisoner of the Goths, the eldest son of this distressed Queen that we may hew his limbs, and on a pile sacrifice his flesh.

SPARK: *(As Tamora.)* Hew his limbs?

SOB: *(As Titus.)* Yes, madam — lop them off like ham-hocks.

SPARK: *(As Tamora.)* Please don't do such a horrible thing to Albert.

SOB: *(As Titus.)* Albert has to die — no, sorry — Ad Manes Fratrum.

SPARK: *(As Tamora.)* Pardon?

SOB: *(As Titus.)* Latin for *"to the spirits of their brothers."*

SPARK: *(As Tamora.)* I don't speak Latin I speak GERMAN.

SOB: *(As Titus.)* My dead son religiously asks a sacrifice and to this your son Albert is mark'd to die and appease my dead son's restless ghost!

SPARK: *(As Tamora.)* Marked? Albert has no marks on him.

SOB: *(As Titus.)* He has to die—

SPARK: *(As Tamora.)* No, he doesn't—

SOB: *(As Titus.)* Yes, he does—

SPARK: *(As Tamora.)* No, he doesn't—

SOB: *(As Titus.)* Yes, he does—

SPARK: *(As Tamora.)* No way—

SOB: *(As Titus.)* He dies, madam!

SPARK: *(As Tamora.)* Victorious Titus, if thy sons were ever dear to thee, O, think my son to be as dear to me!

SOB: *(As Titus.)* You killed my son.

SPARK: *(As Tamora.)* We were fighting a war, idiot!

SOB: *(As Titus.)* Killing is killing.

SPARK: *(As Tamora.)* Yeah, killing is killing, so don't go staining your tomb with my son's blood.

SOB: *(As Titus.)* An eye for an eye, a nose for a nose.

SPARK: *(As Tamora.)* Titus Bouffonius, be merciful: sweet mercy is nobility's true badge.

SOB: *(As Titus.)* We must ask a sacrifice to appease the gods.

SPARK: *(As Tamora.)* What gods?

SOB: *(As Titus.)* The *god* gods — the ones we worship and use to club our enemies with.

SPARK: *(As Tamora.)* Where are they?

SOB: *(As Titus.)* They're up there so you can't see them or maybe you can or maybe they're inside my head or inside yours or maybe we're yearning for Mommy or Mussolini or immortality but nothing's holy in our world, Tamora, even the holes aren't holy — that's why we look to appease the gods even though we are merely their playthings.

ALL: *(Sings.)* O gods, we kneel on broken knees
To appease, appease, appease.
With our Axes and our Swords
Kill a human to keep alive a Lord.

SPARK: *(As Tamora.)* I don't believe in gods — the gods are dead!

SOB: *(As Titus.)* If you don't believe in the gods then you must — at the very least — believe in honour.

SPARK: *(As Tamora.)* Honour? You and your soldiers are rapists, torturers, WORMS — whose honour am I supposed to believe in?

SOB: *(As Titus.)* Your honour, my honour, your son's honour, my son's honour, thus we must honour my son by crucifying yours.

SPARK: *(As Tamora.)* You dishonour the bond between mother and son.

SOB: *(As Titus.)* You dishonour the bond between father and son.

SPARK: *(As Tamora.)* I spit in your face.

SOB: *(As Titus.)* BRING ME THE NAILS!

LEAP: *(As Narrator.)* A soldier brings the nails.

BOOTS: I'LL GET THE NAILS.

*SOB grabs the Albert doll and BOOTS grabs the nails.*

SPARK: *(As Tamora.)* Give him back to me!

SOB: *(As Titus.)* NO!

*SPARK falls on her knees.*

SPARK: *(As Tamora, clutching the Albert doll.)* I beg you, Titus Bouffonius — give back my precious son! I'll protect him from death, I'll protect him from car accidents — he'll grow up big an' strong 'coz I'm his MOMMY.

SOB: *(As Titus.)* Nail him to a cross!

ALL: *(Sings.)* O gods, we kneel on broken knees
To appease, O pretty please—
Kiss our boo-boos, hug our stains
Soothe our throbbing membranes.

SPARK: *(As Tamora, to Titus.)* Fuck all your gods, you merciless piss-flapping dick-weed twat-waffle slug!

SOB: *(As Titus.)* Listen to her blaspheme like a trucker — wait, HOLD IT! I won't crucify her son — it takes too long — I'll just yank off his limbs and peel the muscles off his bones with my own hands.

SPARK: *(As Tamora.)* Nooooooooooooooooooooooooooooo…

*As SOB kills the Albert doll, SPARK makes the sounds of the Albert doll screaming, as well as the sounds of a screaming Tamora.*

SOB: *(As Titus.)* I'm doing this to appease my gods... and it feels good, Tamora, it feels medicinal.

SPARK: *(As Tamora.)* O cruel, irreligious, dishonourable piety!

*SPARK weeps. She is inconsolable.*

SOB: *(As Titus.)* Dear Tamora, it's not personal, it's religious. See how we have perform'd our Roman rites. Albert's limbs are lopped, now let me make my last farewell to my son's soul.

SPARK: *(As Tamora.)* Ahhhhhhh, Albert…

LEAP: *(As Narrator.)* The tomb is opened.

SOB: *(As Titus, sniffs.)* Mmmm, I love the smell of an open tomb. Make way to lay my son by his brethren. There greet in silence, as the dead are wont, and sleep in peace, slain in your country's wars! Here lurks no treason, here no envy swells, here grow no damned grudges…

*SOB weeps again. He and SPARK weep together...loudly.*

SPARK: *(As Tamora.)* Ahhh, my baby, my first born...

SOB: *(As Titus.)* …here no storms, noise, but silence and eternal sleep: in peace and honour rest you here, my sons!

FINK: *(As Narrator.)* Enter Lavinia.

LEAP: *(As Juliet.)* Good night, good night! Parting is such sweet —

SOB: Wrong.

BOOTS: WRONG.

SPARK: WRONG.

FINK: Asshole.

*Exit FINK.*

*Silence...except for BOOTS, who is quietly masturbating with one of Albert's body parts, perhaps a limb.*

SOB: My noble lord and father…

LEAP: *(As Lavinia.)* My noble lord and father, live in fame! O, bless me here with thy victorious hand.

SOB: *(As Titus.)* You look delicious, Lavinia — a bit of icing on your head and you'd be a cake.

LEAP: *(As Lavinia.)* I'm not a cake, Daddy.

SOB: Boots — stop that!

*BOOTS stops masturbating and goes over to SPARK.*

SOB: *(As Titus.)* Lavinia, live; outlive thy father's days and fame's eternal date, for virtue's praise!

LEAP: *(As Lavinia.)* Noble father, the people of Rome have named you in election for the Emperor! O, help to set a head on headless Rome.

SOB: *(As Titus.)* No, a better head her glorious body fits, than his that shakes for age and feebleness — let a younger man campaign for election.

LEAP: *(As Lavinia.)* But who?

SOB: *(As Titus.)* HARK, who comes hitherhere... Saturninus.

*Enter FINK with plastic knives that he hands out to some audience members.*

FINK: *(As Saturninus.)* Countrymen, my loving followers, plead my successive title with your swords: I, Saturninus, am the FIRST-BORN son of the last man that wore the imperial crown of Rome, so let my father's honours live in me — we need no election!

LEAP: *(As Narrator.)* Enter Saturninus armed.

FINK: *(As Saturninus.)* I am entered and I am armed.

*Exit FINK.*

BOOTS: *(As Macbeth, with a brogue.)* Tomorrow and tomorrow and tomorrow creeps—

SOB: Wrong.

SPARK: *(As Tamora.)* Wrong, lover boy, WRONG.

SOB: *(As Titus.)* HARK...Bassianus comes.

LEAP: *(As Narrator.)* Enter Bassianus.

*Enter FINK as Bassianus.*

FINK: *(As Bassianus.)* Friends, Romans, Countrymen, lend me your ears.

BOOTS: WRONG.

SPARK: WRONG.

LEAP: WRONG.

FINK: Fucking idiot — sorry. *(As Bassianus.)* I am Assy-banus — Bassianus, I, Bassianus, am the SECOND-BORN son of the last man that wore the imperial crown of Rome, so let my father's honours live in me. If ever I were gracious in the eyes of Royal Rome, then Romans, fight for freedom in your choice. Demand elections and elect me!

*(As Saturninus.)* There's no need for elections, just choose ME —SATURNINUS! I AM YOUR MAN!

SOB: *(As Titus.)* Please, Princes, calm yourselves.

FINK: *(As Bassianus.)* Beware of Saturninus, whose name starts with SAT for he will SIT on your rights.

ALL: BOO BOO…

FINK: *(As Saturninus.)* Beware of Bassianus, whose name ends in ANUS for he will SHIT on your rights.

ALL: BOO BOO…

FINK: *(As Bassianus.)* Titus, I, Bassianus, do ally in thy uprightness and integrity, and so I love and honour thee and thine and her to whom my thoughts are humbled all, gracious Lavinia, Rome's rich ornament.

*LEAP and FINK make kissy faces at each other.*

FINK: *(As Saturninus.)* Romans, do me, Saturninus, right: draw your swords: and sheathe them not till I becomest Rome's Emperor. Titus Bouffonius, would thou were shipped to hell rather than rob me of the people's hearts!

SOB: *(As Titus.)* No, Saturninus, I'll do my best to restore to thee the people's hearts.

FINK: *(As Saturninus.)* Thank you, Titus.

*(As Bassianus, to Titus.)* Bouffonius, I do not flatter thee but honour thee, and will do until I die.

*(As Saturninus, to Bassianus.)* Your political suck-holing has no place in Roman politics.

*(As Bassianus, to Saturnius.)* You'd suck a sewer if it made you look virtuous.

*(As Saturninus, to Bassianus.)* Bassi-anus Anus ANUS ANUS…

ALL: ANUS ANUS ANUS ANUS ANUS ANUS—

SOB: *(As Titus.)* CITIZENS OF ROME…because I have chosen NOT to wear the Crown, I have been asked to pick the next Emperor…I ask that you create your late Emperor's ELDEST son, Lord Saturnine; whose virtues will, I hope, reflect on Rome as Titan's rays on earth. Take my advice and crown Saturninus and say "Long live our Emperor!"

*BOOTS brings on a paper crown.*

ALL: *(Low, dull.)* Long live our Emperor Saturnine!

FINK: *(As Saturninus.)* LOUDER FASTER BIGGER MORE!

ALL: LONG LIVE OUR EMPEROR SATURNINE. LONG LIVE OUR EMPEROR SATURNINE!

FINK: Better…much better. *(As Saturninus, to everyone.)* Thank you sugar, thank you gods, thank you taxpayers…

ALL: *(Staggered.)* THANK YOU TAX-PAYERS, I LOVE YOU TAX-PAYERS.

FINK: *(As Saturninus.)* …thank you war, thank you peace, thank you paternal bloodline.

*Music as SOB places the crown on FINK… but there is a dust-up around how the crown should sit on FINK's head.*

SOB: *(As Titus, to Tamora.)* Now, madam, you are prisoner to an Emperor. Let him decide what to do with you.

SPARK: *(As Tamora, to Titus.)* Cruel vicious killer — kill yourself for a change.

FINK: *(As Saturninus.)* A goodly lady. Clear up, fair—

SOB: *(As Titus, to Tamora.)* Don't feign innocence, madam — you would have killed one of my sons if our fortunes had been reversed.

FINK: *(As Saturninus, to Tamora.)* A goodly lady. Clear up, fair Green — fair Queen — that cloudy countenance: Though chance of war hath wrought this change of cheer, thou comest not to be made a scorn in Rome: Princely shall be thy usage in every possible physical way — you remind me of my mommy — but never mind, I can make you greater than the Queen of Goths.

SPARK: *(As Tamora.)* Thank you for my freedom—

FINK: It's still my turn… *(As Saturninus.)* Romans, here in Rome we set our prisoners free.

*Someone bangs on something in approval – huzzah, huzzah.*

SPARK: *(As Tamora.)* Thank you for my freedom.

*FINK pulls the chains off BOOTS.*

BOOTS: *(As Aaron.)* I'm not putting those fucking chains on anymore!

SOB & LEAP: *(As Titus and Lavinia, to each other.)* And now we are royally screwed.

FINK: *(As Saturninus.)* Proclaim our honours, Lords, with A DRUM ROLL.

LEAP: *(As Narrator.)* A celebration is in order—

BOOTS: *(As Macbeth, with a brogue.)* Tomorrow and tomorrow and tomor—

LEAP: *(As Narrator.)* A celebration is in order.

ALL: PARTY PARTY PARTY PARTY PARTY PARTY PARTY PARTY...

*Interpretive dance.*

*Exit BOOTS.*

FINK: *(As Saturninus.)* Titus Bouffonius, for thy favours done to me in our election this day, I give thee thanks for electing me, Titus — YOU ELECTED ME!

SOB: *(As Titus.)* There was no election, Lord, I chose you.

FINK: *(As Saturninus.)* YOU ELECTED ME. YOU CHOSE ME — I AM THE CHOSEN! (to Lavinia) And now, to advance thy name and honourable family, Lavinia will I make my Empress, Rome's royal mommy — I mean mistress, mistress of my beating heart, Queen of the World.

LEAP: *(As Lavinia.)* But but—

FINK: *(As Saturninus.)* Tell me, Bouffonius, doth this please you?

SOB: *(As Titus.)* It doth, my Lord.

LEAP: *(As Lavinia.)* But, Daddy, I'm engaged to his brother Bassianus—

FINK: *(As Saturninus.)* To Bassianus? She is damn'd for it!

SOB: *(As Titus.)* My Lord! I will break their engagement.

LEAP: *(As Lavinia, to Titus.)* No, Daddy, no!

FINK: *(To Titus, as Saturninus.)* Traitorous family — if Rome have law or we have power, thou and thy faction shall repent this.

SOB: *(As Titus, to Lavinia.)* I want you to marry Lord Saturninus.

LEAP: *(As Lavinia.)* But Daddy, I love Bassianus—

FINK: *(As Saturninus.)* No, Titus, forget it, the Emperor needs her not, nor her, nor thee, nor any of thy stock.

*Enter BOOTS with the pie that creates a moment of confusion, though FINK continues to huff and puff.*

BOOTS: Here's the pie!

SOB: No, not yet.

*Exit BOOTS with the pie.*

FINK: *(As Saturninus.)* No, Titus, forget it, the Emperor needs her not — fuck no, sorry — no, that's right — No, Titus, forget it, the Emperor needs her not, nor her, nor thee nor any of thy stock so I'll trust, by leisure, him that mocks me once; but YOU, you dishonour me and now you're up shit creek without a paddle. LET IT NEVER BE SAID I BEGG'D THE EMPIRE AT THY MISERLY, TRAITOROUS, BARF-EATING, DAUGHTER-HUGGING, CAKE-LICKING HANDS.

*Exit FINK in a huff.*

SOB: *(As Titus.)* My lord Saturninus! O monstrous! These words are razors to my wounded heart.

*SOB is inconsolable with grief again.*

*Enter BOOTS, still holding the pie.*

BOOTS: *(As Narrator.)* Enter Bassianus.

*Exit BOOTS.*

*Enter FINK as Bassianus.*

*They collide.*

FINK: *(As Bassianus, seizing Lavinia.)* By your leave, Titus, this maid is MINE.

LEAP: *(As Juliet.)* O Romeo! Wherefore art thou Romeo—

SOB: *(As Titus.)* No Bassianus—

FINK: *(As Bassianus.)* Lavinia belongs to me—

SOB: *(As Titus.)* Lavinia belongs to me—

LEAP: *(As Lavinia.)* I belong to myself, Daddy — I'm sexually active and dream of Bassianus licking my coozie.

SOB: *(As Titus.)* Traitor!

*Enter BOOTS without the pie.*

LEAP: *(As Lavinia.)* But Daddy, you know Bassianus and I are engaged.

BOOTS: *(As Narrator.)* Exit Bassianus and Lavinia with Leroy and Todd — oops, sorry.

*BOOTS said the right lines but in the wrong place.*

LEAP: *(As Lavinia.)* But Daddy, you know Bassianus and I are engaged.

SOB: *(As Titus.)* I order you to break your engagement.

LEAP: *(As Lavinia.)* No!

FINK: *(As Bassianus.)* No! "Suum cuique" — it's Latin for—

LEAP: Cunnilingus.

FINK: *(As Bassianus.)* It's Latin for "I seize what I already own."

LEAP: *(As Lavinia.)* We own each other. It's romantic love.

BOOTS: *(As Narrator.)* Exit Bassianus and Lavinia with Leroy and Todd.

*Exit LEAP and FINK, gleefully.*

SOB: *(As Titus.)* HARK — TRAITORS!

SPARK: *(As Narrator.)* Mikey remains behind.

BOOTS: Who's Mikey?

SOB: *(As Titus.)* He's my son. *(To the Mikey doll.)* Mikey, go and bring that young, blind, stupid, sexually disobedient couple back here right this minute!

BOOTS: *(Mikey's voice.)* But Daddy, Lavinia loves Bassianus. She tells me what they do when they're alone and how she fondles his balls — sorry I mean NO, I CANNOT LET YOU PASS, DADDY.

SOB: *(As Titus, to the Mikey doll.)* Mikey, you villainous, pimply-faced masturbating adolescent — when I tell you to do something you do something!

BOOTS: *(Mikey's voice.)* Don't hurt me, Daddy — OW.

*SOB slowly strangles the Mikey doll as BOOTS provides the doll's screams. SOB makes Mikey's little legs kick up and down as the wee doll gasps for air.*

LEAP: *(To everyone.)* Most of these dolls are mine.

*Mikey dies.*

SOB: *(As Titus.)* I have slain my son…ahhhhhhhhh…

*SOB weeps inconsolably.*

*Enter FINK as Saturninus.*

FINK: *(As Saturninus.)* Bassianus and Lavinia have gone — WHY DIDN'T YOU STOP THEM!

SOB: *(As Titus.)* I tried, Lord Emperor King, I did try.

*Perhaps SOB might appeal to the audience for confirmation.*

FINK: *(As Bassianus.)* Fuck you and fuck them. I, Saturninus, am the new Emperor of Rome and can have whomever I wish; therefore, lovely Tamora, if thou be pleased with this my sudden choice, behold, I choose thee for my mommy, and will — sorry — choose thee for my bride, and will create thee Empress of Rome. Squeak — speak, Queen of Goths, dost thou applaud my choice?

SPARK: *(As Tamora.)* I sure do, handsome, and here in the sight of—

BOOTS: *(As Aaron, to Tamora.)* Soon I'll get a chance to mount aloft with thy imperial hotness, mount your pitch—

SPARK: *(As Tamora, to Aaron.)* Wait your turn. *(To Fink.)* I sure do, handsome, and here in sight of heaven, to Rome I swear, if Saturnine advance the Queen of Goths, she will a handmaid be to his desires, a loving nurse, a mommy to his baby parts.

FINK: *(As Saturninus.)* Descend, fair Queen.

SOB: *(As Titus.)* HARK, my Lord, Rome and the righteous heavens be my judge, how I have loved and honoured Saturnine!

FINK: *(As Saturninus, to Titus.)* Go thy way, suck-hole. Thou hast betrayed me.

SPARK: *(As Tamora, to Saturnius.)* My worthy Lord, if ever Tamora were gracious in those princely eyes of yours then hear me out: pardon what is past and stop fighting.

FINK: *(As Saturninus.)* No. First my brother Bassianus stole Lavinia then Titus wouldn't take her back and give her to me — TITUS DISHONOURED ME IN PUBIC! PUBLIC!

SPARK: *(As Tamora, to Saturninus.)* My Lord, Titus loves you — he even killed his son Mikey in loyalty to you so… *(Aside, to Saturninus.)* …smarten up and learn strategy — be nice to them then, yield at entreats; and then let me alone: I'll find a day to massacre them all and raze their faction and their family, the cruel father and his traitorous sons, to whom I sued for my dear son's life, and make them know what 'tis to let a queen kneel in the streets and beg for grace in vain! *(To Titus.)* Come, sweet Emperor; come, dear Titus; kiss and make up.

FINK: *(As Saturninus.)* Rise, Titus, rise; my Empress hath prevail'd.

SOB: *(As Titus.)* I thank your Majesty, and her, my Lord: These words, these looks, infuse new life in me and make me feel less suicidal for having slaughtered my own son. It wasn't my fault my daughter wouldn't break her engagement to Bassianus—

FINK: *(As Saturninus.)* Yes it was!

SOB: *(As Titus.)* No it wasn't!

FINK: *(As Saturninus.)* Yes it was!

SOB: *(As Titus.)* No it wasn't!

FINK: *(As Saturninus.)* Yes it was!

SOB: *(As Titus.)* No it wasn't!

FINK: *(As Saturninus.)* YES IT WAS!

SOB: *(As Titus.)* YES, IT WAS!

FINK: *(As Saturninus.)* NO IT WASN'T!

SOB: *(As Titus.)* YES, IT WAS!

FINK: *(As Saturninus.)* NO IT WASN'T!

SOB: *(As Titus.)* YES, IT WAS!

FINK: *(As Saturninus.)* YES IT WAS!

SOB: *(As Titus.)* NO IT WASN'T!

SPARK: *(As Tamora.)* Titus, I am incorporate in Rome and I must advise the Emperor for his good. THIS DAY ALL QUARRELS DIE — GET IT?

FINK: *(As Saturninus, to Titus.)* Though Lavinia left me like a churle, I've found a friend... *(To Tamora, making naughty insinuations with his plastic knife.)* so come, labia-lips — this day shall be a love-day.

SOB: *(As Titus.)* If it please Your Majesty, let's all go panther hunting tomorrow morning.

SPARK: *(As Tamora.)* That would be lovely, Titus — I love hunting panthers.

*Exit everyone but SOB.*

SOB: *(As Titus.)* Dishonoured thus and challenged of wrongs? What a mess...go ahead, bury Mikey...O my gods, sorrow makes me feel so angry I wish I could bring Mikey back from the dead just so I can kill him again...

*He kicks away the pieces of the Mikey doll.*

SOB: *(As Titus.)* …but I think Tamora will be grateful to me because I was responsible for her sudden rise in status. The gods are just.

ALL: *(Sing.)* The gods are just and will prevail.
As our stupid broken hearts grow frail.
Send down burgers, send down fries,
Consolation for our hungry cries.

SOB: (To audience.) So we've lost Albert and Mikey and now the fun begins as Aaron plots to set up Tamora's sons — Donny and Kevin — to do terrible deeds. Who's driving who to do what? Is Aaron the villain? Is Tamora the villain? Is everyone a villain in some way? Is no one a villain? Here we are in a forest where everyone is going to meet up to hunt panthers but fasten your seatbelts because more than a panther will be hunted.

FINK: *(As Narrator.)* Enter Aaron with a bag of loonies.

*Enter BOOTS carrying a bag of loonies.*

BOOTS: *(As Aaron.)* Hi. I'm Aaron. *(Swats.)* O look, I killed a fly. It feels good to hurt things…slowly. I like pleasure…the pleasure of pain and the pain of pleasure and soon I'll mount aloft with her imperial hotness, mount her pitch then Aaron… then Aaron…

*Silence while BOOTS struggles to find the next line.*

SOB: ...then, Aaron, arm thy heart and fit thy thoughts.

BOOTS: *(As Aaron.)* Then Aaron, arm thy heart and fit thy thoughts to wait upon this new-made Empress — did I say WAIT? No way, I want to WANTON with this Queen, this Goddess — this Nymph will charm the Emperor and I'll rise to him on Tamora's sweet tits.

*Silence.*

SOB: The bag of loonies.

*BOOTS hides the bag of loonies.*

BOOTS: *(As Aaron.)* He that had wit would think that I had none, to bury so many loonies under a tree, and never after to inherit it. But alas, I have a strategy, which, cunningly effected, will beget a very excellent piece of villainy: and so repose, sweet bag. *(Listens.)* HARK…who comes? Tamora's sons, Donny and Kevin.

*Enter SPARK holding the Donny and Kevin dolls.*

SPARK: *(As Kevin.)* Donny, I plead my passions for Lavinia's love.

*(As Donny.)* Kevin, I plead MY passions for Lavinia's love.

*(As Kevin.)* No, I plead MY passions for Lavinia's love.

*(As Donny.)* NO, I PLEAD MY PASSIONS FOR LAVINIA'S LOVE.

BOOTS: *(As Aaron.)* Why, how now, Lords! Are you comparing passions?

SPARK: *(As Kevin.)* I love Lavinia more than all the world.

*(As Donny.)* I love Lavinia more than all the world.

BOOTS: *(As Aaron.)* Both of you could take her — one from the front, one from the rear.

SPARK: *(As Kevin.)* Faith, not me. I love her eyes too much.

*(As Donny.)* Faith, not me, I adore her nose.

BOOTS: *(As Aaron.)* Adore her nose, ha ha — she wouldn't look twice at your muffin-faces. She and Bassianus are engaged, so the only way you could have Lavinia would be to rape her.

SPARK: *(As Kevin and Donny.)* No, that's cruel, that's so cruel and…you mean just ask her if she'll let us finger her lady parts?

BOOTS: *(As Aaron.)* Don't ask her. Rape is power and it's a very bad thing to do but it feels good while you're doing it unless the person you're doing it with pulls out a knife and cuts off your manly parts then you're nothing but a particle of uselessness watching the seconds fall off your life.

SPARK: *(As Kevin and Donny.)* ...Wow.

BOOTS: *(As Aaron.)* My lords, the forest walks are wide and spacious; And many unfrequented plots there are fitted…*(struggles to remember line)*… plots there are fitted for fun…for…

SOB: *(To BOOTS.)* ...fitted by kind for rape and murder…"

BOOTS: …fitted by kind for rape and murder, there serve your lusts, shadow'd from heaven's eye, And revel in Lavinia's treasury which I suspect is full of sparkle.

SPARK: *(As Kevin.)* Yeah, Lavinia's treasury.

*(As Donny.)* Yeah, Lavinia's sparkly treasury.

BOOTS: *(As Aaron.)* Hark, your mommy's coming — go hunt some panthers.

SOB: *(As Narrator.)* Exit Donny and Kevin.

*SPARK tosses the Donny and Kenny dolls.*

SPARK: *(As Tamora.)* My lovely Aaron—

BOOTS: *(As Macbeth, with a brogue.)* Tomorrow and tomorrow and tomorrow—

SPARK: Wrong — we're not doing that one, how many times I gotta tell you. *(As Tamora.)* My lovely Aaron, wherefore look'st thou sad, when everything doth make a gleeful boast?

BOOTS: *(As Aaron.)* No, madam, vengeance is in my heart, death in my hand. Let me avenge the death of... of your son Aidan — Allan—

SPARK: Albert.

BOOTS: *(As Aaron.)* Albert. Let thy sons make pillage of Lavinia's chastity and wash their hands in her blood. Here, take this note and give it to Emperor Saturninus. It says, "If thou dig a grave for Bassianus and toss him in, then look for thy reward over near the tree — a bag of loonies."

*BOOTS drops the note on the ground so that SPARK has to bend over in order to pick it up...and immediately they begin humping.*

SPARK: *(As Tamora.)* Ah, my sweet man, sweeter to me than life!

BOOTS: *(As Aaron.)* You bet — oh mommy mommy make me purr.

SOB: *(As Narrator.)* Enter Lavinia.

BOOTS: *(As Aaron.)* No more; we are espied.

SOB: *(As Narrator.)* Enter Lavinia.

*Enter LEAP.*

LEAP: *(as Lavinia)* Who have we here?

BOOTS: *(As Aaron.)* No more; we are espied.

*Exit BOOTS.*

LEAP: *(As Lavinia, to Tamora.)* Who have we here? Rome's Royal Empress alone in the woods kissing another man?

SPARK: *(As Tamora.)* Unmannerly intruder! Where's Bassianus?

LEAP: *(As Lavinia.)* He's gone to pick flowers for me. Daffodils are my favourite.

SPARK: *(As Tamora.)* Get lost, kitten — go join the hump — the hunting party.

LEAP: *(As Lavinia, touching Tamora's belly.)* Did you swallow a balloon or are you pregnant?

SPARK: *(As Tamora.)* Why have I patience to endure this?

LEAP: *(As Lavinia.)* I wish I could be pregnant. Bassianus and I want a boy and a girl or maybe two girls — they can have Pink Ears and No Feet or Lime Fingernails with Red Noses and Yellow Hair.

SPARK: *(As Tamora, calls.)* Donny? Kevin? Get over here!

SOB: *(As Narrator.)* Enter Donny and Kevin again.

*Enter BOOTS with the Donny and Kevin dolls.*

BOOTS: *(As Donny.)* Oh Lavinia…hello there, beautiful.

SPARK: *(As Tamora, to her sons.)* I have been severely insulted.

LEAP: *(As Lavinia, to Tamora.)* Can I touch your tummy again?

BOOTS: *(As Donny.)* Whoever severely insults my mother severely insults me.

SPARK: *(As Tamora, re: Lavinia.)* This one has called me foul adulteress and lascivious Goth.

LEAP: *(As Lavinia, to Tamora.)* I'm sorry I insulted you — I just really like talking about sex and babies.

SPARK: *(As Tamora, to her sons.)* Revenge it, as you love your mother's life, or be ye not henceforth call'd my children!

BOOTS: *(As Donny.)* This is to prove that I am your son.

SOB: *(As Narrator.)* Donny grabs Lavinia.

BOOTS: *(As Kevin.)* And this is to prove that I'm your son, too.

SOB: *(As Narrator.)* Kevin gropes Lavinia.

LEAP: *(As Lavinia.)* O Tamora! Help me—

SPARK: *(As Tamora, to her sons.)* I will not hear her speak — away with her!

LEAP: *(As Lavinia.)* O Tamora, be called a gentle queen and stop this or kill me yourself.

SPARK: *(As Tamora.)* So should I rob my sweet sons of their fee: No, let them satisfy their lust on thee. *(To her sons.)* The more you make her suffer, boys, the better I'll feel — AWAY WITH HER!

LEAP: *(As Lavinia.)* ... someone please help me pleeeeeeeeeeeeeeeeeease...

*Exit LEAP with the Donny and Kevin dolls.*

*SPARK listens to LEAP's loud screams and the grunting and humping sounds of Donny and Kevin.*

*After a few moments, two plastic cut-off bleeding hands are tossed onto the stage.*

*Enter FINK with some daffodils.*

FINK: *(As Bassianus.)* Lavinia, my love...

SPARK: *(As Tamora.)* Bassianus.

FINK: *(As Bassianus.)* How now, where is Lavinia?

SPARK: *(As Tamora.)* Picking daffodils — they're her favourite flowers.

FINK: *(As Bassianus.)* Who was screaming…is that Lavinia? Hark, what's this… *(Examining one of the cut-off hands.)* …Lavinia...is this your dear hand? *(To Tamora.)* Where is she hither? Where is the rest of Lavinia?

SPARK: *(As Tamora.)* I don't know — I wasn't here.

FINK: *(As Bassianus.)* The new incompetent unelected Emperor shall hear about this outrageous fortune and take up arms against a sea of troubles — no sorry — wait 'til I tell him I saw you in the forest with another man, I can only imagine what you two were doing — rubbing your private parts, fucking with astonishing abandon and rapidity…*(He uses Lavinia's hand to rub against his groin, then he starts to cry.)*…kissing each other and O Lavinia, my dearest love… where are you?

*FINK, as Bassianus, is inconsolable… licking Lavinia's severed hands and crying.*

*Enter BOOTS with a plastic knife covered in something red, and the Donny and Kevin dolls.*

BOOTS: *(As Kevin.)* Wow, that was fun.

*(As Donny.)* Yeah, we cut out her tongue and chopped off her hands so she can't identify us.

*(As Kevin.)* Awesome strategy — I should be the Emperor, eh, Mom?!

SPARK: *(As Tamora, to her sons.)* Yes, you should be, Donny, and now that you've finished raping Lavinia, I have another chore for you... *(Lowers her voice.)* Bassianus threatened to tie me up then let a thousand toads and hissing snakes attack me so I'd die a miserable death. Had you not arrived right this second I would be dead! Revenge this, too — we are drowning in vengeance today but REVENGE IT!

ALL: *(Sing.)* Revenge is the sugar in my blood
The acid in my dirty shame,
It's the ache inside my burnt-out heart,
The screaming infant in my brain.
Sorrow is the stink between my sheets
The smelly inflammation of my cage,
It's the free coffee I toss back in your face
The mushroom pizza I shit on in my rage.

*An interpretive dance might be performed here (or not) while FINK sobs.*

*BOOTS — holding the Donny and Kevin dolls — sneaks up behind FINK who is hunched over, and the dolls stab him to death.*

FINK: *(As Bassianus.)* I don't want to die like this; I don't want to die, period.

BOOTS: *(As Aaron.)* Throw his body into the pit.

*BOOTS and SPARK have some trouble rolling FINK's body over.*

SPARK: *(As Tamora.)* I must take this letter to Saturninus. *(To FINK.)* You weigh a ton — musta gobbled down twenny hamburgers for lunch, eh?

BOOTS: *(As Aaron.)* I must...I must find Titus' sons and bring them hither...because revenge is the sugar in my blood, wet and loud like a screaming baby.

*Exit SPARK and BOOTS…then FINK gets up and exits.*

*Enter LEAP…no hands and something red on her lips and face.*

LEAP: *(As Lavinia.)* Ow I hur I hur... ("Ow I hurt I hurt…")

*She spits out her bloody tongue then begins to cry inconsolably…*

*Enter SPARK, holding the Donny and Kevin dolls.*

SPARK: *(As Kevin.)* Hey Lavinia, try singing "Twinkle, Twinkle, Little Star."

LEAP: *(As Lavinia, sings.)* in gle, in gle, ital ar ho... ("Twinkle, twinkle, little star, how…")

SPARK: *(As Donny.)* Look, Ma — no hands?

*LEAP runs through the audience calling...*

LEAP: Hel…911 caw 911 caw 911... ("Help...911 call 911 call 911…")

*Exit LEAP.*

*Exit SPARK with the Donny and Kevin dolls.*

*Enter BOOTS with the Leroy and Todd dolls.*

BOOTS: *(As Aaron.)* Come along, Leroy and Todd. Do you want to impress your daddy Titus by catching a panther? Look right down into the pit…do you see the panther?

*(As Leroy and Todd.)* …oh wow whoa…what's that?

*(As Aaron.)* A panther. You want to get a closer look? Look closer, closer…

*BOOTS rolls the two dolls on the ground.*

SOB: *(As Narrator.)* Leroy and Todd are pushed into the pit…

BOOTS: *(As Todd.)* Eek eek…Lord Bassianus lies dead in a heap like to a slaughter'd lamb, in this detested, dark, blood-drinking pit.

*(As Leroy.)* Oh wow — get me outta here!

*(As Macbeth, in a brogue.)* Awake, awake! Ring the alarm bell. Murder and treason!

*(As Aaron, still in brogue, calls)* HELP HELP THERE'S BEEN A TERRIBLE ACCIDENT. THREE PEOPLE ARE IN A HOLE AND ONE IS DEAD.

SOB: *(As Narrator.)* Enter the Emperor, Lord Saturninus.

FINK: *(As Saturninus.)* What's going on? What hole is here and who's in the hole?

*BOOTS picks up the Todd and Leroy dolls.*

BOOTS: *(As Todd and Leroy.)* The unhappy sons of Titus found your brother Bassianus — dead.

FINK: *(As Saturninus.)* My brother…dead?

BOOTS: *(As Todd and Leroy.)* We know not where you left him all alive; but here have we found him dead.

FINK: *(As Saturninus.)* What? My brother dead! 'Tis not an hour since I left him alive—

BOOTS: *(As Todd and Leroy, lost, repeats line.)* We know not where you left him all alive; but here have we found him dead.

FINK: *(As Saturninus.)* What? My brother dead! 'Tis not an hour since I left him alive—

BOOTS: *(As Todd and Leroy.)* We know not where you left him all alive—

*Enter SPARK and SOB.*

SPARK: *(As Tamora.)* Where is my Lord the Emperor?

SOB: *(As Titus, looking for Lavinia.)* Speak, gentle daughter, what stern ungentle hands have lopped and hewed and made thy body bare of her…Lavinia?

*Puzzlement.*

*SOB said the right lines but in the wrong place.*

SOB: Oops — too soon.

SPARK: *(As Tamora.)* Where is my Lord the Emperor?

FINK: *(As Saturninus.)* Right here, Tamora, though grieved with killing grief. Poor Assy-banus — Bassianus — he lies here murdered and now I have no family left.

*FINK is inconsolable.*

FINK: I wish Mommy were here to hug me and make me a bowl of soup — sorry. *(As Saturninus.)* I wish I had a bag of loonies to pay for Bassianus' funeral.

SPARK: *(As Tamora, remembers the note and hands it to FINK.)* Almost too late I bring this fatal writ — the complot of this timeless tragedy.

FINK: *(As Saturninus, reads.)* "If thou dig a grave for Bassianus and toss him in, then look for thy reward over near the tree — a bag of loonies." O Tamora, was ever heard the like?

BOOTS: *(As Aaron, picking up the bag of loonies.)* My gracious Lord, here is the bag of loonies and here is the pit — Todd and Leroy are guilty of killing Bassianus.

*They all look into the "pit."*

SOB: *(As Titus.)* My dear sons…

*FINK sees Todd and Leroy then picks up the two dolls.*

FINK: *(As Saturninus, to Todd and Leroy.)* YOU TWO WHELPS HAVE HERE BEREFT MY BROTHER OF LIFE — (To Titus.) ARREST THEM AND DRAG THEM TO PRISON. THERE LET THEM BIDE UNTIL WE HAVE DEVISED SOME NEVER-HEARD-OF TORTURING PAIN.

BOOTS: *(As Aaron.)* Yippee, more pain — MORE HARD-CORE PAIN.

*SOB makes his "son" dolls — Todd and Leroy — scream "Nooooo…let us explain." Then he grabs both of the dolls and clasps them tight to his heart.*

SOB: *(As Titus, to Saturninus.)* Lord King Emperor, upon my feeble broken knees and with tears not lightly shed, my sons are innocent until proven guilty. I wish to post their bail.

FINK: *(As Saturninus, to Titus.)* There will be no bail for these little pecker-heads! *(To Todd and Leroy.)* Do not speak a word, boys — your guilt's as clear as the noses on your faces. *(To Titus.)* Your sons Todd and Leroy will be crucified at dawn — hung on a cross until dead dead dead DEAD!

*FINK grabs the Todd and Leroy dolls from SOB.*

BOOTS: I'LL GET THE NAILS.

SOB: *(As Titus.)* What? No, dear Emperor, no — I'll pay double bail, triple...O my gods, this cannot be happening...

SPARK: *(As Tamora.)* Titus, don't worry, dear warrior... *(Fondles Titus.)* I'll work my magic on the King; fear not thy sons; I'll get them out of this mess.

SOB: *(As Titus.)* I need a moment alone to collect my thoughts.

BOOTS: *(As Narrator.)* Exit all but me, Aaron, his dignity and rage intact.

*Puzzlement.*

SOB: Exit all but me.

BOOTS: *(As Narrator.)* Exit all but me.

SOB: All but ME, Titus.

BOOTS: *(As Narrator.)* Exit all but ME, Titus...his dignity and rage intact.

*Exit all but SOB, who begins to cry. He is inconsolable.*

SOB: ...Narrator and Saturninus and Music?

*Music.*

*Enter SPARK, FINK and BOOTS. SPARK carries the cross and a hammer, FINK carries the Todd and Leroy dolls, and BOOTS carries the pie.*

SPARK: *(As Narrator.)* Rome. A street. *(To BOOTS.)* No, not the pie — not yet.

*Exit BOOTS with the pie.*

SPARK: *(As Narrator.)* Todd and Leroy are bound on the way to be crucified.

*FINK makes Todd and Leroy scream.*

SOB: *(As Titus.)* Lord Emperor King God Saturninus, a dribble of pity for me whose life has been spent fighting for Rome whilst you slept securely on fluffy pillows; I lost twenty-one sons on the battlefield and only have three sons left.

LEAP: *(Offstage.)* TWO.

SOB: Pardon?

LEAP: *(Offstage.)* TWO SONS LEFT AND A DAUGHTER — ME!

SOB: Thank you. *(As Titus.)* O merciful Lord, unbind my sons, reverse the doom of death — can't you see I'm crying my eyes out?

*Enter BOOTS with nails.*

FINK: *(As Saturninus.)* Cry me a river, you shit-kissing bum-gobbler. I, who shine with Titan's rays on earth, pronounce your sons Todd and Leroy guilty of murdering my brother Bassianus.

BOOTS: I brought the nails.

*FINK makes the dolls — Todd and Leroy — scream again "Nooooo…"*

SOB: *(As Titus.)* Saturninus, Lord Emperor, King of the World, once more I entreat you to please…fuck you, I'm tired of begging. Fuck all of you.

FINK: *(As Saturninus.)* Fuck you, too.

SPARK: *(As Tamora, to Titus.)* Yeah, eat shit suck dick go fuck a moose.

FINK: *(As Saturninus.)* The crucifixion starts in five minutes — FREE PARKING!

*Exit SPARK, BOOTS, and FINK with the dolls.*

SOB: *(As Titus.)* Rome is but a wilderness of tigers. Tigers must prey and Rome affords no prey but me and mine. Hark, who comes here…?

*Enter LEAP, no hands and no tongue.*

SOB: *(As Titus.)* O no! Speak, gentle daughter, what stern ungentle hands have lopped and hewed and made thy body bare?

LEAP: *(As Lavinia.)* Yay waped me… ("They raped me.")

SOB: *(As Titus.)* What?

LEAP: *(As Lavinia.)* Yay waped me… ("They raped me.")

SOB: *(As Titus.)* They raped you?

LEAP: *(As Lavinia.)* ya. Er eh uck air eenis i eye ellee uc-on en eye ee-air a eye ag-ina a eye a-us A UP AME IME. ("First they stuck their penises in my belly button then my ear then up my vagina and my anus AT THE SAME TIME.")

SOB: *(As Titus.)* But, sure, some jerk hath deflowered thee, and now thou turn'st away thy face for shame!

LEAP: *(As Lavinia.)* A way it. ("A rape kit.")

SOB: *(As Titus.)* I am dishonoured by your shame — what will people think of me?

LEAP: *(As Lavinia.)* A way it. ("A rape kit.")

SOB: *(As Titus.)* Lavinia, whoever raped and silenced you, raped and silenced me, too.

LEAP: *(As Lavinia.)* A WAY IT! ("A RAPE KIT.")

SOB: *(As Titus.)* Who raped you?

LEAP: *(As Lavinia.)* A way it. ("A rape kit.")

SOB: *(As Titus.)* Who?

LEAP: *(As Lavinia.)* A WAY IT. ("A rape kit.")

SOB: *(As Titus.)* Ape shit?

LEAP: *(As Lavinia.)* OOO — WAY IT. ("NOOO — RAPE KIT.")

SOB: *(As Titus.)* A rape kit?

LEAP: *(Nods.)* Yaaaa. ("Yeah.")

SOB: *(As Titus.)* DOES ANYONE HAVE A RAPE KIT? There's blood coming out of your mouth — did they rape you in the mouth, too?

LEAP: *(As Lavinia.)* uck ow my ung... ("Cut out my tongue.")

SOB: *(As Titus.)* They cut out your tongue?

*LEAP opens her mouth wide and SOB looks into it.*

SOB: *(As Titus.)* O gods, I feel sick — who did this?

LEAP: *(As Lavinia.)* on ee a eev-iin. ("Donny and Kevin.")

SOB: *(As Titus.)* My wretched sons are condemned to die, but that which gives my soul the greatest spurn is dear Lavinia, dearer than my soul.

*LEAP weeps. SOB holds her and weeps. They weep together, inconsolable.*

*Enter BOOTS.*

BOOTS: *(As Aaron.)* Titus Bouffonius, my Lord Emperor sends thee a message that, if thou love thy two sons, Leroy and Todd, chop off your hand and send it to the King and he'll return your sons to you. It's a good deal — two sons for the price of one hand.

SOB: *(As Titus.)* O gracious, gentle Aaron, thank you.

BOOTS: *(As Aaron.)* Don't suck up to me, buddy.

SOB: *(As Titus.)* With all my heart, I'll send the Emperor my hand: good Aaron, wilt thou help to chop it off?

BOOTS: *(As Aaron.)* Gimme your paw…

*BOOTS takes out her plastic knife and starts to saw off SOB's hand.*

*SOB tries not to scream.*

BOOTS: *(As Aaron, to Lavinia.)* Close your eyes, lovely, 'coz this is going to be exquisitely painful. Your father's screams of agony will get me so excited I might lose control of my passionate nature and—

SOB: *(As Titus.)* Shut up — do it fast!

*SOB screams. LEAP screams.*

BOOTS: *(As Aaron.)* This knife is really dull.

SOB: *(As Titus.)* DO IT FASTER.

*LEAP tries to kick BOOTS.*

BOOTS: *(As Aaron.)* I don't want to ruin the meat.

SOB: *(As Titus.)* FASTER.

BOOTS: *(As Aaron.)* It's not easy to cut through bone.

ALL: *(Sing.)* Willingly we suffer for our children
To keep their tiny little silly hearts alive.
We brave the tortures of the damned
To hold and kiss their dirty sticky hands
And pray our darling perfect children will survive.

SPARK: *(As Narrator.)* Aaron cuts off Titus's hand.

*SOB screams as BOOTS cuts off SOB's hand.*

SOB: *(As Titus, to Aaron.)* Give His Majesty my hand. Tell him it was a hand that warded him from a thousand dangers; bid him bury it and give me back my sons.

BOOTS: *(As Aaron.)* I go, Bouffonius, and for thy hand look by and by to have thy sons with thee. *(Aside.)* Their heads, I mean. O, how this villainy doth FAT me...soon there will be pie!

*Exit BOOTS.*

*SOB raises his hand up to the heavens.*

SOB: *(As Titus.)* O, here I lift this one hand up to heaven, and bow this feeble ruin to the earth: if any power pities wretched tears, to that I call!

SPARK: *(As Narrator.)* Enter Aaron.

BOOTS: *(As Aaron.)* Hey, Titus, I got a message for you from the Emperor. As promised, he's returning your two sons...

*BOOTS tosses the heads of Titus's two sons at SOB.*

BOOTS: *(As Aaron)* ...and here's your hand.

*BOOTS tosses SOB's hand.*

*Exit BOOTS.*

SOB: *(As Titus.)* COME BACK HERE YOU MANIACAL LYING CHEATING SON OF A SHITBAGGING WEASEL. WHEN I GET MY HANDS — HAND — ON YOU I'LL…

*SOB slowly picks up the severed heads of his sons and his own severed hand.*

*Silence…then he begins to laugh.*

SOB: *(As Titus.)* I have not another tear to shed.

LEAP: *(As Lavinia.)* I ill ah uckers. I ill ah uckers. ("I'll kill the fuckers.")

SOB: What fuckers — who are you talking about?

*LEAP is trying to pull something out from between her legs but has trouble grasping it. She tries to get SOB to help.*

LEAP: *(As Lavinia.)* Ul a scing...a scing... ("Pull the string.")

*He looks and sees the string. He yanks on it and she grabs it with her stumps and pulls out a big red bloody tampon.*

SOB: *(As Titus.)* Daughter, did those boys do something to your head — do that in the bathroom. Gross me out...oh dear, I can't believe you did that…

*Holding the tampon with her stumps, LEAP uses it to write on the floor, occasionally dipping it back into herself for more "ink."*

SOB: *(As Titus.)* …O bloody period, I'm going to faint… what are those…are those letters...? Soft! See how busily she writes! D o n n v — no — is that a V or a Y? Y. K e v — Donny and Kevin — did they do this to you?

LEAP: *(As Lavinia, nods.)* Yes.

SOB: *(As Titus.)* Those disgusting wank-faced toads and their slobbering genitalia — what's happening? We've become an Empire of Sorrow, a Nation of Rage, of Fear — a Herd of Pornographic Warriors in the Age of Unreason — did I fight for this degradation? Did I fight for my daughter to be raped and mutilated? Did I fight for my sons to be crucified without proof they committed a crime? Did I fight for a government run by a man whose anus...yeah, I did. I chose him. Why? What did I really want? Was I blind, was I crazy, was I too modest, too proud? Did I want to be liked more than I wanted to be wise? Why didn't I take the fucking crown when it was offered me but oh no, instead of taking the crown I killed my son Mikey I KILLED MY OWN SON AS I WOULD SWAT A FLY and oh, I fear...I fear the souls of the children I murdered will come for me in the night. I've tried to be fair — fair? Gimme a fucking break — we got nothing at The Society For The Destitute 'cept paper plates and plastic knives and hardly any books — in one of the richest countries we got nothing but someone else's charity and I don't want charity, I want meaning because I gave and gave — I thought I was giving myself to help build the future but I was just filling someone else's treasure chest to support someone else's corruption to feed someone else's power, it's always someone else's power — kings, prime ministers, presidents, dictators, billionaires, gods *(To the sky.)* "Ruler of the great heavens, are you so slow to see crimes?" Tamora was right — FUCK THE GODS! REVENGE IS THE ONLY GOD WE WILL WORSHIP FROM NOW ON, LAVINIA!

LEAP: *(As Lavinia, suffering.)* I hur…ow ow ("I hurt...ow ow.")

SOB: *(As Titus.)* How could they do this to you — maybe I should just kill you and put you out of your misery.

LEAP: *(As Lavinia.)* O o... ("No no...")

SOB: *(As Titus, fighting off tears.)* Sorrow blinds me and I fear revenge is the only solace, but I cannot find the way to Revenge's cave. These two heads are saying "Daddy, go to Revenge's cave — GO." They're shouting "Revenge's Cave is the gaping hole in our necks," and revenge is the gaping hole in your eyes, Lavinia, and it beckons me, it beckons us…I feel an overwhelming urge to crucify someone — it's rising inside me it's rising—

LEAP: *(As Lavinia, struggles to speak to the world with no tongue.)* eye odd-ee is-ent er odd-ee...my body isn't your body — nothing in the world gives you the right to touch my body — I'm the only one who gives you that right 'coz I'm the Boss of My Body — the only right you have is to bow and say, "O Majestic Boss, could I touch your body" an' if I say yeah then you can touch my breasts, kiss my nipples, but those two fucker-heads didn't have any right to touch me so as punishment from me — the Boss — I'm sending out this order: Before those boys are crucified I'm gonna cut their cocks off an' shove 'em down their throats then make 'em sing "Twinkle, Twinkle, Little Star" while they're bleeding out an' I'm gonna sue that thunder-cunting Queen for encouraging her sons to rape me!

*SOB picks up balloons and a magic marker.*

SOB: *(As Titus.)* That's my girl — come, let's send those boys a gift — a gift of words.

*Exit LEAP.*

SOB: *(To the audience.)* And now we're in the thick of things. So far six people are dead — Albert, Mikey, Todd, Leroy, Bassianus — sorry, five — and one has yet to be born…which leaves nine more to be killed, including the clown.

FINK: There's no clown.

SOB: *(To the audience.)* Yes, thank you. There's no clown in our adaptation, but soon the clown will be dead even though the clown is not in my adaptation. Moving right along, Titus is determined to take revenge, so he comes up with an idea to undermine the King and Queen…then the fun begins.

*Enter SPARK — very pregnant — and BOOTS.*

SPARK: *(As Narrator.)* A room in the Emperor's palace. Aaron watches Tamora who is in labour.

*SPARK squats down and suffers as she gives birth. A huge grunt and scream as she pulls out a black baby doll from between her legs.*

BOOTS: *(as Aaron)* O wow, is that MY child, my baby? Is it a girl—

SPARK: *(As Tamora, to Aaron.)* Shut up. Go find me a white baby — no. Shut up and take this baby.

*BOOTS fastens her eyes on her child — it's love at first sight.*

BOOTS: *(As Aaron.)* Ahhh…my son…coochy coo coochy coochy coo. What shall we name him?

SPARK: *(As Tamora.)* Nothing. Go christen him with thy dagger's point.

BOOTS: *(As Aaron.)* Why would you murder our son?

SPARK: *(As Tamora.)* The Emperor will kill me if he ever finds out about us — and I got a good thing going here so yeah, kill the baby — better to kill a kid than let 'em get entangled in fuckin' Children's Aid 'coz Children's Aid can fuck a life.

BOOTS: *(As Aaron.)* Whoever touches this my first-born son and heir dies upon my dagger's sharp point because I'm keeping my darling baby boy.

SPARK: *(As Tamora.)* Go find me a white baby and I'll tell Saturninus it belongs to him.

BOOTS: *(As Aaron.)* Ye white-limbed walls, ye fucking white people, coal black is better than another hue. Who else besides your sons, Donny and Kevin and myself know about our son?

SPARK: *(As Tamora.)* The Nurse.

BOOTS: *(As Aaron, calls.)* Bring in the Nurse.

SPARK: Delivering a kid sure gives yer hoo-ha a bloody workout.

*Enter FINK with the Nurse doll.*

SPARK: It's like taking a gargantuan shit.

BOOTS: *(As Aaron, to the Nurse.)* Nurse, how many people saw my baby?

FINK: *(As the Nurse, high voice.)* Just me, the Nurse. That black baby is a joyless, dismal — sorry, not black like...that baby is a joyless, dark — sorry, not dark but that black, sorry, baby of colour is you know... uh, can I say this, mixed race babies make the CUTEST babies...like you have a race baby and you have a normal baby and you mix 'em together an' yeah, sorry sorry...here in the hospital we care and have respect for all people — for all colours of people like they matter, you know, like white people they matter — I'm sure you know that — and red people they matter — (well they're not really red...) all people uh black lives they matter but like even, I don't know, like blue lives, they matter, you know what ALL LIVES MATTER!

SOB: *(As Narrator.)* AARON KILLS THE NURSE.

FINK: *(As the Nurse, high voice.)* I'm not racist — it's the lines — Shakespeare's a racist, not me — it's his words. I have lots of Black Canadian-African Afro-Albertan friends — DOCTORS!

*BOOTS moves towards FINK.*

FINK: *(As the Nurse, high voice.)* You know the ones that — fuck what? WHAT? You can't make racist jokes anymore? You know what — I'm calling this, I'm calling this: I FEEL UNSAFE. What about me? WHAT ABOUT ME?

BOOTS: *(As Aaron.)* IT'S NOT ABOUT YOU — IT'S NEVER ABOUT YOU PEOPLE — IT'S ABOUT THE AFFAIR AND ME KILLING YOU TO HIDE IT BUT NOW YOU'RE DOUBLE DEAD 'COZ YOU JUST COMMITTED SOCIAL DEATH!

FINK: *(As the Nurse, high voice.)* I did?

BOOTS: Yeah, fuckface — look at how they're looking at you.

*Silence as FINK makes the Nurse doll look around at the audience...then the Nurse realizes...*

FINK: *(As the Nurse, high voice.)* ...oh my god...

*Suddenly FINK makes the Nurse doll break her own neck.*

FINK: *(As the Nurse, high voice.)* O, I die.

BOOTS: NO, DON'T — I was just trying to — FUCK! WHY DO THEY ALWAYS DO THAT?

*FINK tosses the Nurse doll.*

SPARK: Some women say pushing out a kid gets them hot — I had five an' lemme tell you I didn't ever get hot 'coz it hurt like torture the whole time 'specially when you get torn to pieces — my third — Ricky, a nine-pounder — ripped me from vag to anus. You talk about anus anus — I coulda built Rome right up inside me there—

SOB: OK, enough jerking off.

SPARK: Don't fucking silence me — I'm up to telling my birthing stories.

BOOTS: I wanna be born from you.

SPARK: Yeah, that's what they all say.

FINK: So do I — I want to be born from you.

SPARK: See.

LEAP: That Black baby doll isn't one of my dolls.

SOB: FROM THE NARRATOR'S LINE "AARON KILLS THE NURSE."

FINK: *(As Narrator.)* AARON KILLS THE NURSE. Exit everyone but Aaron and his baby.

BOOTS: *(As Aaron, to the baby.)* I'll take you home to the Goths, as swift as the swallow flies. I'll make you feed on berries and roots, and suck the goat, and bring you up. I will name you Boots the Second and raise you up to be a Great Warrior 'coz I'm your daddy.

*Exit BOOTS with the doll.*

SPARK: *(As Narrator.)* Titus and Lavinia in a Pubic — Public Place.

*Enter SOB and LEAP holding plastic knives with balloons attached. The balloons have messages scrawled on them.*

SOB: *(As Titus.)* I made Rome miserable when I supported Saturninus' bid for Emperor — it was a brain malfunction on my part. It's time to take our country back. Lavinia! *(Reads a balloon message.)* This balloon says, "The Emperor is a fascist." *(Reads another balloon message.)* "Saturninus picks his nose and eats it." "Our Emperor sleeps with dictators." "Saturninus kisses corporate ass." "Swamp the Drain."

LEAP: *(As Lavinia.)* SWAMP THE DRAIN SWAMP THE DRAIN—

SOB: You have to stop talking — you have no tongue.

LEAP: I'll only stop talking if I can have a nice death at the end of this play.

SOB: OK.

LEAP: If I were Juliet I could die so beautifully...

SOB: Shush. *(As Titus.)* Toss your balloons into the Emperor's courtyard!

*They toss the balloons.*

LEAP: ...die with love on my lips, die with my lips on fire.

*Exit SOB and LEAP.*

BOOTS: *(As Narrator.)* Meanwhile...in the Emperor's courtyard.

*Enter FINK as Saturninus, picking up one or two of the balloons, and SPARK carrying the Donny and Kevin dolls.*

FINK: *(As Saturninus.)* Titus Bouffonius is crazy — *(Reads.)* "Saturninus sucks Goths." — spreading all this cack-cack poo-poo — message balloons flying around the streets of Rome! Trashing me, libelling me against the Senate, proclaiming our injustice everywhere, making fun of my afflictions — spreading rumours that I'm an orphan and dress my pet sheep in evening gowns — now the citizens of Rome will end up hating me and loving him! I want him crucified for treason — NOW!

SPARK: *(As Tamora.)* My gracious Lord, lovely Saturnine, Master of my life, Commander of my thoughts, Master Commander of my Heart, King Commander Master of my Master Commander King — calm the fuck down. Titus is old and he's sad about losing three of his sons. I have him where I want him, caught between revenge and revenge, ripe for the killing...soon he'll walk into my trap and my — our future will be golden.

*SPARK picks up one of the balloons and reads the message written on it.*

FINK: *(As Satuninus, reads.)* "The Emperor only wipes his bum on Sundays." O my gods, that is so insulting and mostly not true. Titus is mean — as if his traitorous sons that died by LAW FOR THE MURDER OF MY BROTHER HAVE MY BY BEANS — sorry — HAVE BY MY MEANS BEEN BUTCHERED WRONGFULLY. Bring me Bouffonius so I can rip him apart with my own two bare hands—

SPARK: *(As Tamora.)* If you want Titus to stop his smear campaign, why not invite him to dinner so you two can kiss and make up—

FINK: *(As Saturninus.)* Do not interrupt me when I am speaking. *(Big breath.)* OK, I'm finished speaking.

SPARK: *(As Tamora.)* ...why not invite Titus to dinner so you two can kiss and make up or — even better — we'll poison his food — yeah, I'll put poison in the cookies and permanently end this balloon mischief.

FINK: *(As Saturninus.)* He'll never come to our palace for dinner.

SPARK: *(As Tamora.)* O yes, he will. We just have to come up with a plan to lure him here.

FINK: *(As Saturninus.)* I'm too stressed to think. Give me another blow job then I wanna breast-feed for a little while.

SPARK: *(As Tamora, aside.)* Why are men in power so much work? I want my revenge, my castle and gold without having to babysit a quivering mass of jelly. *(To Saturninus.)* Dearest Emperor, the eagle suffers little birds to sing, and is not careful what they mean thereby, knowing that with the shadow of his wings, he can at pleasure stint their melody, so put your eagle face on, lover-boy, and think positive.

FINK: *(As Saturninus.)* OK. If I kill myself now, do you think I'll go down in history as the greatest Emperor Rome has ever seen?

SPARK: *(As Tamora.)* Lord King, I have a better idea…like me, Titus will want revenge for the death of his sons…so I'll pretend to be Revenge and lure him to our place for dinner…*(aside)* it involves a skeleton.

FINK: *(As Saturninus.)* Tamora...I fear the souls of those two children I murdered might come for me in the night.

SPARK: *(As Tamora.)* Nah…

*Exit SPARK and FINK.*

SOB: *(To the audience.)* The body count builds — the Nurse and the non-existent Clown — are both dead. That's seven down, seven to go. Tamora decides to trick Titus into coming for dinner so she can poison him. Soon she will dress up as the character of Revenge and dress up her sons Donny and Kevin as Rape and Murder…but first Titus goes after Aaron who ran away from Rome after falling in love with his baby son — no, not the incest kind of love — the true kind of love that parents have for their children. And now…who will be the next to die?

*(As Narrator.)* On the Plains near Rome. Aaron sings a lullaby to his baby.

BOOTS: *(As Aaron, sings.)* "Lullaby and good night, go to sleep and sleep tight, close your eyes, close your nose…"

*Enter SOB…who walks up behind BOOTS and grabs the baby doll from her.*

SOB: *(As Titus.)* Hands up!

BOOTS: *(As Aaron.)* HEY — THAT'S MY BABY!

SOB: *(As Titus.)* Your baby's dead dead DEAD — and so are you for setting up the murder of my two sons!

BOOTS: *(As Aaron.)* Go ahead — kill me — but please save my baby. His name is Boots the Second and he's of royal blood! I'll give you the dirt on Tamora so you can destroy her, then impeach Saturninus — but first swear my baby shall live. Pick a god you can swear to.

SOB: *(As Titus.)* I don't believe in gods anymore, so you better start talking or you're going to be writing an obituary for Boots the Second.

BOOTS: *(As Aaron.)* OK OK, I begot this child on the Empress; helped her sons Donny and Kevin kill Bassianus and roll him into the pit; lured your sons Todd and Leroy to the pit and pushed them in; hid the bag of loonies and wrote the letter Saturninus found; urged Donny and Kevin to ravish your daughter; played the cheater for your hand and laughed extremely loud when your two son's heads rolled out — and when I told the Empress she laughed, too and gave me twenty lovely licks.

SOB: *(As Titus.)* Your psychotic lack of remorse is shocking, disgusting and traumatizing, but also quite impressive.

BOOTS: *(As Aaron.)* I've done a thousand dreadful things as willingly as one would kill a fly, and nothing grieves me heartily indeed but that I cannot do ten thousand more.

SOB: *(As Titus.)* Start walking back to Rome. Away with you, inhuman dog, unhallowed slave! Try anything funny and I'll smash Boots the Second so hard he'll swallow his own neck.

BOOTS: *(As Aaron.)* OK you white maggot — I'm walking.

*Exit BOOTS holding Boots the Second.*

SOB: *(As Titus, aside.)* ...Ah, I am so full of sorrow that I want to kill the world.

*Exit SOB.*

FINK: *(As Narrator.)* Outside Titus' house.

*Enter SPARK as Tamora holding a life-sized skeleton in front of her, with the Donny and Kevin dolls attached — in some fashion — on either side of the skeleton, on the shoulders or the arms.*

SPARK: *(As Tamora, calls.)* Hello, Titus Bouffonius…

*Enter SOB, inconsolable.*

SOB: *(As Titus.)* Who doth molest my contemplation of suicide?

SPARK: *(As Tamora.)* I am come to talk with thee, Titus Bouffonius.

SOB: *(As Titus.)* I'm not in the mood for conversation; besides, you sound like that bitch Tamora.

SPARK: *(As Tamora.)* She is your enemy, but I am your friend.

SOB: *(As Titus.)* Art thou Revenge?

SPARK: *(As Tamora.)* Yes, I am Revenge and these are my ministers Rape and Murder.

SOB: *(As Titus.)* O sweet Revenge, help me kill the Empress.

SPARK: *(As Tamora.)* I'll arrange a banquet for you at the Emperor's palace and bring in the Empress, her sons, and all thy foes.

SOB: *(As Titus, aside.)* They think I'm crazy but I recognize them — a pair of cursed hellhounds and their cunning mommy! *(To Tamora.)* I'd rather have the dinner at my place.

SPARK: *(As Tamora.)* We have a marble dining table with one-of-a-kind veining.

SOB: *(As Titus.)* I like to cook.

SPARK: *(As Tamora.)* I love to cook.

SOB: *(As Titus.)* I love to cook more than you — MY PLACE OR NOTHING!

*In the background, BOOTS is gleefully holding up the pie.*

SPARK: *(As Tamora.)* OK, darling, it's a date. Now I'll take my leave and take my ministers with me.

SOB: *(As Titus.)* Let Rape and Murder stay and keep me company. Vengeance is a lonely place, as you well know.

*SPARK removes her doll sons from the skeleton and FINK takes over the manipulation of Donny and Kevin.*

SPARK: *(As Tamora.)* Farewell, Bouffonius. See you at dinner — I'll bring dessert.

*Exit SPARK.*

SOB: *(As Titus.)* Lavinia, come here.

*Enter LEAP.*

SOB: *(As Titus.)* Do you know these two?

LEAP: *(As Lavinia.)* You bet your buttons I do — those are the fuckers who hurt me.

SOB: *(As Titus.)* Let's crucify them.

FINK: *(As Donny and Kevin.)* No no mommy mommy help me mommy.

LEAP: *(As Lavinia, jumping up and down.)* CRU-CI-FY THEM, CRU-CI-FY THEM…

ALL: CRU-CI-FY THEM, CRU-CI-FY THEM!

BOOTS: I'LL GET THE NAILS.

LEAP: I'LL GET THE WOOD.

SPARK & FINK: I'LL GET THE BUCKETS!

SOB: *(As Titus.)* Oft you have heard me wish for such an hour, and now I find it, therefore nail them sure, and stop their mouths if they begin to cry.

*As SOB, BOOTS and LEAP nail the dolls to the cross in real time, FINK makes the dolls cry and scream and SOB does his speechifying.*

LEAP: Most of these dolls are mine.

SOB: *(As Titus.)* Hark villains, Kevin and Donny! We're crucifying you so you'll suffer and bleed into our buckets, and when you're almost dead we'll cut you down and grind your bones to powder and with your blood and it'll make a delicious...say it now, Boots.

BOOTS: P I E! P I E!

SOB: *(As Titus.)* Let's make these little fuckers cry.

*They all bear the dead dolls on the cross and sing.*

ALL: *(Sing.)* Willingly we suffer for our parents
To keep their silly awful adult hearts alive.
We brave the suffering of the damned
To hold their large warm venomous hands
And pray our darling perfect parents won't survive.

LEAP: *(As Lavinia.)* The worst revenge is the best revenge.

*Exeunt all but SOB.*

SOB: *(To the audience.)* Two more dead…that's eight, no nine, and five more to go for a grand total of fourteen. Revenge is a snake that eats its tail and shits it out then eats that same shit and shits it out again and again and again. It must taste good.

*Enter SPARK and BOOTS, who is holding the pie.*

SPARK: *(As Narrator.)* Titus' house. A banquet is set out.

BOOTS: Here's the pie — straight out of the oven!

SPARK: *(As Narrator.)* Enter Titus, Lavinia, Aaron and his baby. Aaron is in chains.

BOOTS: *(As Aaron.)* In these fucking chains. Again.

*Exit SPARK.*

*Enter SOB, wearing an apron or a chef's hat, and LEAP. They set up ketchup bottles, paper plates, plastic forks, knives and forks and flowers are arranged.*

SOB: *(As Titus.)* Our guests should be here soon.

LEAP: *(As Juliet.)* Romeo, Romeo, wherefore art thou…

SOB: You have no tongue.

LEAP: I know I have no tongue I KNOW I HAVE NO TONGUE, YOU DON'T HAVE TO KEEP TELLING ME — *(In tongue-less garble.)* US COZ I AVE O UN GOES EN EEE I AUN EEK.

*Enter FINK and SPARK.*

SOB: *(As Titus.)* Hark, dear Lord Emperor and Empress, welcome to my table. I've been cooking all morning.

FINK: *(As Saturninus.)* I don't eat potatoes, string beans, or pork and I have an aversion to purple lettuce.

SPARK: *(As Tamora.)* I'm allergic to shellfish, marshmallows, frozen peas and I don't like leeks.

SOB: *(As Titus.)* Please you, therefore, draw nigh, and take your places. Happily there are no potatoes, no beans, no pork and no purple lettuce, no shellfish, no marshmallows, no frozen peas or leeks — just meat and gluten-free rice.

SPARK: *(As Tamora.)* I love the flower arrangement. Daffodils are my favourite.

LEAP: *(As Lavinia.)* ine oo. ("Mine too.")

SPARK: *(As Tamora.)* We brought delicious pois — delicious regular cookies for dessert.

SOB: *(As Titus.)* Thank you, dear Queen. Though my food be plain, it'll fill your tummies. Bene spiat! That's Latin for bon appetit which is French for "good appetite" which is English for "down the hatch."

FINK: *(As Saturninus.)* We are beholden to your hospitality, Bouffonius. Let today mark the day we rekindle our friendship for our mutual political goats — goals.

SOB: *(As Titus.)* Yes, today is the first day of the rest of our lives.

SPARK: *(As Tamora.)* You're quite a good cook.

SOB: *(As Titus.)* Cooking calms me down.

SPARK: *(As Tamora.)* Mmmm…this is tasty. Nice and beefy.

SOB: *(As Titus.)* They were busy animals, slaughtered in their prime.

BOOTS: *(As Aaron, breaking the chains.)* These chains are such bullshit.

FINK: *(As Saturninus.)* There's a hint of garlic and something…something bittersweet, leaning more toward the bitter.

SOB: *(As Titus.)* My Lord Emperor, answer me this: If you were going to eat a baby, where would you start?

*A moment.*

SOB: *(As Titus.)* Sorry — that was awful. Sorry.

SPARK: *(As Tamora.)* What's awful is that I actually started thinking of an answer.

FINK: *(As Saturninus.)* I already have an answer.

SPARK: If you're after asking me about eating some of the Children's Aid staff I wouldn't hafta even think — I'd be munchin' on their fuckin' faces before they could blink—

SOB: *(As Titus.)* My Lord Emperor, answer me this: do you think a father should slay his daughter because she was raped?

FINK: *(As Saturninus.)* Yes, absolutely.

SOB: *(As Titus.)* Why?

FINK: *(As Saturninus.)* Because the girl should not survive her shame, and by her presence still renew her father's sorrows.

SOB: *(As Titus.)* If performing such a thing would free me from my sorrow then die, die, Lavinia, and thy shame with thee.

*SOB grabs a ketchup bottle, raises a plastic knife and tries to kill LEAP.*

LEAP: *(As Lavinia.)* No, Daddy, no!

*LEAP hits SOB with her flowers.*

LEAP: *(As Lavinia.)* I'm not ashamed.

SOB: *(As Titus.)* But I'm ashamed.

LEAP: *(As Lavinia.)* It's not my fault her sons did this to me so I'M NOT ASHAMED!

FINK: *(As Saturninus.)* Whose sons?

SOB: *(As Lavinia.)* You're supposed to die silently.

LEAP: *(As Lavinia, points to Tamora.)* Hers — Donny and Kevin.

SOB: *(As Titus.)* Lavinia!

FINK: *(As Saturninus, to Tamora.)* Is that true?

SPARK: *(As Tamora.)* No. She's crazy.

LEAP: I WILL NOT DIE SILENTLY — GIMME THE KNIFE.

*She grabs the knife out of SOB's hand.*

SOB: HEY!

LEAP: THIS WASN'T PART OF OUR DEAL. I WANT MY DEATH — I WANT MY BEAUTIFUL DEATH.

FINK: *(As Saturninus, to Lavinia, re: knife.)* Careful where you're pointing that thing.

LEAP: *(As Juliet.)* Thy lips are warm.

SOB: *(As Titus.)* Give it back, Lavinia!

LEAP: *(As Juliet.)* Yea, a noise?

SPARK: *(As Tamora.)* See, she's crazier than a bag of hammers.

LEAP: *(As Juliet.)* Then I'll be brief. O happy dagger, this is thy sheath. There rest and let me die.

*LEAP stabs herself and dies beautifully, graced with lots of ketchup.*

LEAP: *(As Lavinia.)* O...I...die.

FINK: *(As Saturninus.)* Unnatural and unkind — what hast thou done?

SOB: *(As Titus.)* I meant to put her out of her misery and temper my grief but then she killed herself… now my grief is made a thousand times worse.

SPARK: *(As Tamora.)* Grief is a cancer, best to cut it out.

SOB: *(As Titus.)* I fear the souls of our murdered children will come for us in the night.

FINK: *(As Saturninus.)* Nonsense. Children are like fish — they don't feel pain or remember anything 'til they're forty then they go into therapy to search for their mommy's face and confront the soul-destroying fragility of their broken — sorry.

SPARK: *(As Tamora.)* Most fish don't live past forty 'less they're Blue Whales.

FINK: *(As Saturninus, to Titus.)* So, Lavinia was ravish'd — who did the deed?

SOB: *(As Titus.)* You heard her — Kevin and Donny raped her and cut out her tongue.

FINK: *(As Saturninus, to Titus.)* Die, frantic wretch, for this accursed deed!

*FINK said the right lines but in the wrong place.*

FINK: Oops, sorry.

SOB: *(As Titus.)* You heard her — Kevin and Donny raped her and cut out her tongue.

SPARK: *(As Tamora.)* You have no proof!

FINK: *(As Saturninus, to Tamora.)* Go fetch your sons so they can prove their innocence.

SOB: *(As Titus.)* No need to fetch them. They are already here.

SPARK: *(As Tamora.)* They're here — where?

SOB: *(As Titus.)* Baked in that pie whereof their mother daintily hath fed, eating the flesh that she herself hath bred.

SPARK: *(As Tamora.)* …I'm going to puke…

FINK: *(As Saturninus.)* He's just joking. That's a damned cruel joke, Titus.

SOB: *(As Titus.)* I'm not joking…here's Kevin's toe.

SPARK: *(As Tamora.)* Ahhhhhhhhhhh…

SOB: *(As Titus.)* An eye for an eye, a nose for a nose, a toe for a toe…

SPARK: *(As Tamora.)* You killed my sons — THREE OF THEM.

SOB: *(As Titus.)* You killed TWO OF MINE.

SPARK: *(As Tamora.)* You killed one of your sons BY YOUR OWN HAND.

FINK: *(As Saturninus, to Titus.)* Your sons killed my brother Bassianus.

SOB: *(As Titus.)* No they didn't — HER sons killed your brother and it was this sick puppy with the baby who set them up!

BOOTS: *(As Aaron.)* I'm not sorry.

FINK: *(As Saturninus, to Aaron.)* Die, frantic wretch, for this accursed — what an idiot — sorry.

BOOTS: *(As Aaron.)* I'm not sorry.

SPARK: *(As Tamora.)* I ate my sons…help me, I'm dying.

FINK: *(As Saturninus, to Aaron.)* Did you set up Tamora's sons to kill my brother?

BOOTS: *(As Aaron.)* I'm innocent until proven innocent.

SOB: *(As Titus, to Tamora.)* Here have more — have the whole pie!

FINK: *(As Saturninus, to Aaron.)* Answer my question!

SOB: *(As Titus.)* Where's my knife?

BOOTS: *(As Aaron.)* If one good deed in all my life I did, I do repent it from my very soul.

*SOB stabs SPARK…ketchup and more ketchup.*

FINK: *(As Saturninus, to Aaron.)* As Emperor of Rome, I shall have you crucified at dawn — *(Then, trying to stop Titus from killing Tamora.)* hey HEY!

SOB: *(As Titus, to Tamora.)* You're not getting any funeral, Tamora — no funeral, no formaldehyde, no flowers!

SPARK: *(As Tamora, dying.)* Emergency call 911...call 91... O, I die.

*SPARK dies.*

SOB: *(As Titus, to Tamora.)* Good. I'm gonna bury you in a dumpster beside a dead dog.

LEAP: I want a dog — a live one — a Dalmatian.

SOB: You're dead!

FINK: *(As Saturninus, to Titus.)* Die, frantic wretch, for this accursed deed!

*FINK starts stabbing SOB and SOB stabs him back — fatally — then SOB, dripping in ketchup, grabs the crown and puts it on his own head.*

SOB: *(As Titus, to Saturninus.)* And I'm gonna put a dead dog on your face, you fascist piece of shit.

FINK: *(As Saturninus, dying.)* I'm allergic to dogs…

LEAP: I'm not allergic to dogs.

FINK: *(As Saturninus, dying.)* …thank you, taxpayers. Mommy, where are you… O, I die.

*SOB makes a grab for Boots the Second, but Aaron scoops the doll up in her arms.*

BOOTS: *(As Aaron.)* DON'T TOUCH MY BABY!

*FINK dies as SOB goes after BOOTS… and they are equally matched, plastic knife against plastic knife, both equally fatally wounded. A ketchup storm.*

SOB: You're supposed to die.

BOOTS: I will die — but I'm going down heroic. *(As Macbeth, with a brogue.)* Tomorrow and tomorrow and tomorrow creeps…

*SOB stabs BOOTS.*

BOOTS: O, I die…

*BOOTS dies. SOB picks up Boots the Second to kill him…but instead he — SOB — starts to slowly fall down...*

SOB: *(As Titus.)* Alas, I'm fatally wounded…a tooth for a tooth, an arm for an arm…hand for a… decapitated head for a de ca pi ta…O…I… die.

*SOB dies…*

*...then the ghost babies begin to appear. Many, many dolls can be seen, their ghostly white bodies suspended in the air. These are the souls of children who were killed, and they have come back to haunt the living and the dead. They cry.*

*Below, Boots the Second is alive. He cries the loudest.*

*Darkness.*

*Lights come up. FINK, SOB, SPARK, BOOTS and LEAP get to their feet.*

*The End*

The Society for the Destitute Presents Titus Bouffonius

Words by Colleen Murphy
Music by Mishelle Cuttler

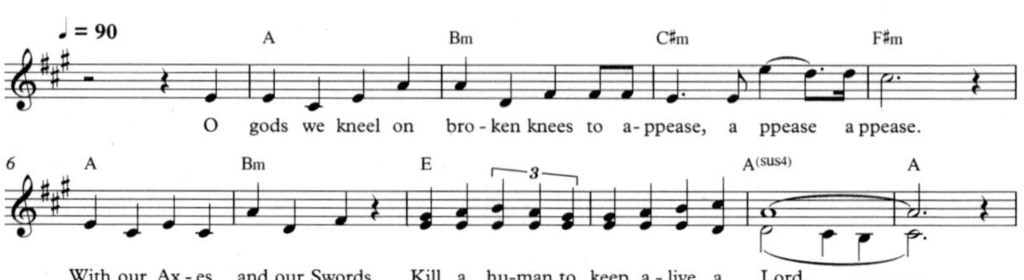

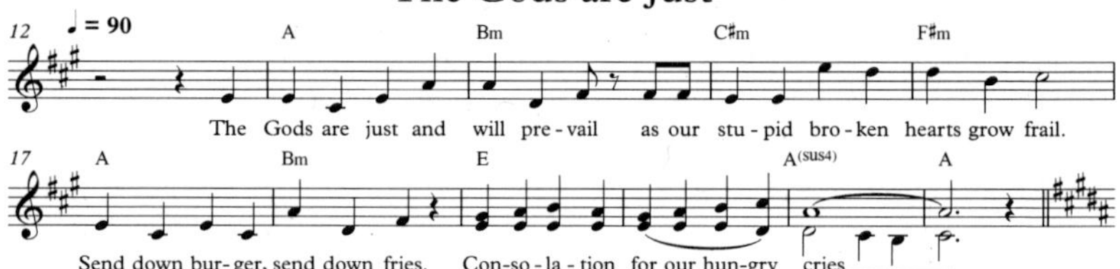

The Society for the Destitute Presents Titus Bouffonius

Words by Colleen Murphy
Music by Mishelle Cuttler

## Suffer for Our Children

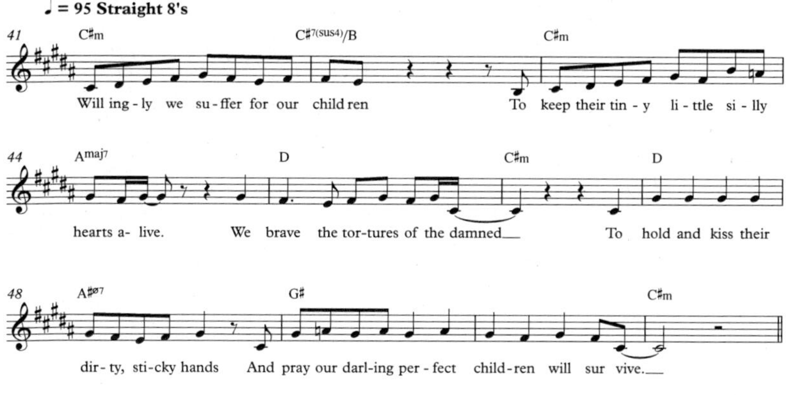


## Suffer for Our Parents